The Warrior Bride

JOANNA ALONZO

Mahal Kita, Pilipinas.

Contents

Author's Note

DEAR READER,

This book is somewhat of a paradox. It was strangely both the easiest and hardest book to write in this series of devotionals.

It was easier, because unlike the first two in the series, I stepped into this with a rough plan. I still based the story of the warrior princess/bride on whatever God was impressing me to write on the particular day it was written, but there was more of a pattern followed in that I divided the forty days into the lives of eight women in the lineage of Christ (with the exception of Esther, who represents the Bride). The eight women are: *Eve (Cursed), Tamar (Betrayed), Rahab (Desperate), Ruth (Grieved), Bathsheba (Shamed), Leah (Unwanted), Mary (Risked),* and *the Bride (Betrothed).* Through glimpses of their stories, I wanted to show some of the things we fight against as Christians in this world.

The hard part was in the subject matter itself. While *The Woman in the Wilderness* and *The Kingdom Child* drew largely from my personal experiences, this devotional is more about the things I am challenging myself with. It came out of a season of me feeling like I had to contend for my destiny, like His promises were slipping away from me, and I was missing out, and I needed to fight for it if I wanted to stay at the center of His will.

In a lot of ways, even after having written and released this book, I still feel that way. I will probably feel that way

— like I have to keep contending — until Christ returns. After all, the days are growing ever darker, but we take heart, because in great darkness, His great light can shine through.

I pray you find within the pages of this devotional the faith to fight the good fight to the very end. May it stir up within you the urge to contend for God's promises for your life, your family, your home, your city, your nation, and the rest of the world.

Shalom and Mabuhay!

Blessings,
Joanna Alonzo
www.joannatheparadox.com

A.F.T.L.

to the warriors,
contending for their destiny

Fight the good fight of faith, lay hold on eternal
life, to which you were also called and have
confessed the good confession in the presence
of many witnesses.
1 Timothy 6:12 (NKJV)

acknowledgments

Thanks to my parents, June and Rose Alonzo, for never giving up on me and for contending for my life and purpose from the moment of my birth to this very day.

To Janna, my sister, for continuing to shine her light in the midst of darkness. May her light ever grow brighter and transform more lives, bringing them to the glory of God's salvation.

To my Risen Savior, the Lover of my soul, may You find in this book, the work of my hands, an act of worship unto You, an offering with a pleasing aroma rising to Your throne.

IX

introduction

YOUR MISSION

You have experienced the kingdom of God. You have been among His people, gathered with them, communed with them, been wounded by them. The kingdom child has learned to love and be loved by God and by His other children. You belong to His family of believers, and you have embraced your role in it, a role that sometimes requires you to lead and to feed the lambs — His sheep — whom He has entrusted to you. His kingdom is beautiful, and you rejoice in your part in it. However, there is yet a mission at hand — a mission you must accomplish. You can't just remain in His kingdom among His people.

You are tasked with advancing His kingdom. To be light in darkness.

For that to happen, you obey His call to step in the darkness as His light, a candle that must maintain its flame no matter how the fickle winds of the world blow.

To reach the fullness of who you have to become to be counted among the Bride of Christ, you must first be tested in the crucible of suffering, where your resolve is melted, your heart allowed to break, so you could be made whole again.

Ultimately, you arise a warrior.

One who can take a stand for righteousness amid persecution, trials, and suffering. One willing to brave the darkness, trusting His glorious light will keep shining in you and through you.

The days are dark and hatred grows.

Scripture speaks of a bride who is ready, one who has been given authority to tread on serpents and scorpions. It remains a mystery to you what it means to exercise such authority. You wonder what price you must pay, what sacrifice must be made for you to emerge out of trial and temptation, a warrior bride.

So, despite not knowing, you follow the Commander of the angel armies, the One Whom you know as Beloved and King. He is the Leader you are willing to follow anywhere.

If these words are true of you, if it awakens in you a desire to rise a warrior, brave in heart, and loyal to the King of Glory no matter the cost, the Warrior Princess being molded to become a Warrior Bride is you.

I pray this book will stir in you a hunger and thirst for righteousness, as well as a strong sense of identity, destiny, and purpose, so when the enemy tries to steal your inheritance and birthright as the King's Beloved, you know how to contend for what the King has said is rightfully yours. May this devotional expand your heart for the lost, for the captives, for those who yet need to hear the Good News of the Kingdom of God. I pray that in her dive into the darkness as an ambassador of light, The Warrior Bride will awaken in you the understanding and wisdom necessary to prepare for the return of the King, so that in His return, you will be among those ready to fight, and ready to rule and reign with Him.

We shine with Him. We battle with Him.

Until we reach the complete manifestation of the victory Christ has won at the cross.

Contend, Warrior Bride.

day 1

City of Darkness, City of Light

A traveling band of ten among the children of light — seven children and three of age — treaded the grounds of a city under the rule of the enemy. The flicker of a rainbow, the sign of a covenant-keeping Ruler, had given them hope they could get through the mysterious city and reach the capital of their Great King.

Formerly a woman in the wilderness and forever a kingdom child, the warrior princess led her small group of those seeing and hearing past the city of darkness, which, most unexpected to her, didn't appear dark at all. On the contrary, it was full of color and light, with people rushing around them, to and fro, heading who knows where.

A growing dread slowly diluted their group's fascination. Was the city they had walked into as it seemed? Why was there an underlying current of something sinister hiding in the shadows, waiting to pounce on them?

A slither, already far too familiar to her, snickered at her. _What are you doing here, child?_

She didn't respond. Her ancient foe wasn't worthy of her time.

It's not what you expected, isn't it? You thought you were walking into a city of darkness and desolation. Yet, here you are, surrounded by a city of light and freedom. Don't you see? Your King lied to you. The world beyond His kingdom's borders, outside His rule, isn't dark at all. We have our own light. We have our own glory.

"It's not what I expected," her companion and friend, the sentinel, said to her.

The warrior princess sighed. "Sometimes, we cannot rely only on what we see. We need to look beyond what's in front of us. Stay on guard."

"I agree." The iron maiden, their fellow sojourner, nodded.

The warrior princess smiled.

"What?" The iron maiden widened her eyes.

"The three of us rarely agree unanimously on something."

"Well, we are no longer in a kingdom surrendered to the King." The iron maiden's eyes darted from side-to-side, vigilant as they walked farther into the territories of a city unknown to them. "We cannot afford to be divided."

"I will stand guard over the group from behind," the sentinel volunteered. He made his way behind their group to protect their wards — the mission God had entrusted to them — from the back. The iron maiden walked alongside the children, taking on the middle flank.

The warrior princess blinked at her surroundings, the bright lights straining her eyes. They needed to find shelter in this strange city. Where were they to stay?

An immediate answer to her unspoken question, a woman covered from head-to-foot by a scarlet cloak covering everything but her face approached them. "It's you!" she exclaimed. "Finally!" She covered her eyes when she reached them.

Something about the urgency in the woman's tone and the eagerness by which she greeted them gave the warrior princess peace. "We are from the kingdom of light," she said to the stranger.

"I am the daughter of enmity." She squinted her eyes and blinked as if she was having trouble seeing them. "Please. Follow me. We must get out of here. I will explain later."

The warrior princess looked back at her fellow leaders. Both nodded their agreement, so they followed the daughter of enmity onto a bright highway. After they had already gone about a third through the empty highway, the warrior princess turned to check on their group only to gasp in surprise. Behind them, the city of bright lights was now shrouded in darkness.

Only then did she realize. As usual — true to its eternal nature — the words that came out of the slither's hiss were nothing but lies. The city wasn't a city of light. It was them. They were the light, and wherever they went, they radiated their King's glory.

Manna

Verses for Meditation

Eve — Cursed: *Now the serpent was more crafty than any of the wild animals the Lord God had made. He said to the woman, "Did God really say, 'You must not eat from any tree in the garden'?"*
Genesis 3:1

*See, darkness covers the earth
and thick darkness is over the peoples,
but the Lord rises upon you
and his glory appears over you.*
Isaiah 60:2

When Jesus spoke again to the people, he said, "I am the light of the world. Whoever follows me will never walk in darkness, but will have the light of life."
John 8:12

Author's Reflections

As children of light, it should no longer surprise us to find ourselves in a world shrouded in darkness. We live in times where the world applauds what Scripture says to be wrong and shames what Scripture says to be righteous. This dichotomy will only increase as the coming of the Lord draws near.

In it all, we remember we are children of the day tasked to bring His light and love wherever we are. There are many among us called to go to specific places where darkness rules and evil thrives. There are also those who are to stay at the home front supporting those who go, but still keeping the fire blazing where they have been instructed to stand guard. Whichever of the two you are — maybe both, depending on the season — you have a part in the Great Commission.

Today, let us look beyond what we are going through, and ask God to reveal to us a nation or a people who yet need to hear the Gospel. Find someone to agree with you in prayer and pray for the salvation of this nation or people group, as well as His grace, blessing, protection, and wisdom upon our brothers and sisters who are standing as representations of Christ's light among them.

day 2

THE LIE THAT BROKE HER

Whichever road they treaded, lights flickered open. What they left behind slowly dimmed but didn't completely embrace the darkness; somehow, remnants of their essence stayed to provide embers of light. What would happen if wherever they went, they kindled a fire? Would it die or shine forever?

The daughter of enmity rushed forward, the hem of her cloak sweeping the pavement beneath her. She led them into a ramshackle establishment, which was more ruin than building, as if it had been ravaged by war.

She opened a door tattered and boarded up — like it had been broken into multiple times — and ushered them inside a simple apartment, larger on the inside than it appeared from the outside.

Her eyes still strained at the sight of them, but it didn't take long before she got used to their light. The iron maiden volunteered to look after the children while the warrior princess and the sentinel helped their host prepare a meal.

"I once was a daughter of light," the daughter of enmity said as she brought out bread and butter from a well-stocked pantry. "I was a caretaker, tasked with looking after and further cultivating some of the most vibrant and breath-taking gardens you can imagine. In the kingdom of light, beauty and peace surrounded me.

Here, my neighbors are hostile toward me. I am constantly derided and attacked."

The sentinel's brows creased. "Why?"

"I am the daughter of enmity. I am opposed by both light and darkness, and if I am to be honest with you, I can't blame anyone but myself. It is my curse, one that I brought upon myself by the choices I've made."

The warrior princess placed bread in a basket while the sentinel prepared a pitcher of milk. They exchanged glances, both perturbed by what their host was talking about.

"I don't understand. How are you being opposed by both sides?"

Their host sighed as she transferred fruits from a basket onto a wooden bowl. "I am detested by citizens of this city for having once been a daughter of the light. They will show the same hostility to you, but it won't be the same hostility they show me."

"Why is that?" the warrior princess asked.

"You never dared believe you could be ruler of all, like I did. The prince of darkness once lied to me. He told me he loved me, cared about me, and if only I would leave the kingdom of light and serve him, I will be powerful, ruling the kingdoms by his side. I shouldn't have believed him. The King of light has been good to me, but I gave in to the prince's allure. I joined him in his city, and for a while, it satisfied me, but only as long as it took for the light within me to fade away and succumb to the darkness surrounding me. The prince threw me out. Without my light, I was no longer appealing to him. Just another one of his conquests." She stared at the bowl of fruit between her hands and forced a smile. "I'm sorry. You did not travel all the way here to listen to my woes. Let us eat."

With a lump in her throat, the warrior princess carried the bread and butter into the dining area, her heart broken over the daughter of enmity's story. Surely, there was a way to restore her to the light! If there was, the warrior princess would find it!

Manna

VERSES FOR MEDITATION

EVE — CURSED: *"You will not certainly die,"* the serpent said to the woman. *"For God knows that when you eat from it your eyes will be opened, and you will be like God, knowing good and evil."*
Genesis 3:4-5

The mind governed by the flesh is hostile to God; it does not submit to God's law, nor can it do so.
Romans 8:7

"I have told you these things, so that in me you may have peace. In this world you will have trouble. But take heart! I have overcome the world."
John 16:33

AUTHOR'S REFLECTIONS

We are, unfortunately, born into a world of enmity. This has been so since the day Eve believed the lie of the serpent and took a bite of the forbidden fruit. The world is growing hostile toward Christians, because the flesh seeks its own pleasure, its own satisfaction and fulfillment. It is against our sinful nature to follow the Word of God, and the enemy doesn't hesitate to use this against us.

Yet, we have a God who gives us His shalom, His supernatural abiding nature if we only ask Him for it, if we only continue to seek Him and obey Him — by His grace alone! — and trust in His promise that we will overcome.

He has overcome the world. In Him, so can we.

THE FRUIT SHE HAD PARTAKEN

A hush filled the table where a spread of bread, fruit, and milk was waiting for them. The iron maiden expressed gratitude on their behalf for rest after a long journey and for a meal to strengthen them as they move forward past the great city and to a kingdom they all were yearning for.

As the iron maiden said thanks to the King, tears rushed down the daughter of enmity's eyes.

The warrior princess grabbed hold of her hand and squeezed. Was there hope yet for her? Surely there was! How could there not be? Was one such as her, having once turned her back on the King, no longer welcome in the kingdom of light?

Starving, as soon as the iron maiden's prayer was over, their group broke bread and ate. The warrior princess picked a bright red apple and took a bite from it, its sweetness satisfying her taste buds.

"Are you not going to eat?" the warrior princess asked their host.

"The meal was sent specifically for you. The King's subjects still come to this city — there are many of them here, much to the disdain of the prince. That is why we are not completely lost in darkness. There are many yet who have found His light but choose to remain in the city, so they could keep kindling a flame, hoping the fire would catch and many more would embrace the light."

"And you?" the iron maiden asked. "Do you not crave the light?"

"When one has been in darkness for a prolonged period, light becomes painful. It burns. I have been a friend of darkness for far too long, I'm afraid."

"And yet—" the sentinel narrowed his eyes at her "—you still welcome the King's children in your home."

"A gesture of gratitude toward a King Who once took care of me and fed me, who still sends His children to provide for me. Maybe if I keep caring for His children, He will remember how I once cared for His gardens. Perhaps He will remember me."

"I doubt He has forgotten you," the warrior princess said.

As soon as the words came out of her lips, the slither came. <u>Lies! She has partaken of the fruit I offer. One such as her can never again be a daughter of light. Why do you give her false hope?</u>

The warrior princess shook her head to cast the voice of darkness out of her ears. She held on to her host's hand. "If you seek the King with all your heart and your soul, you will find Him. I once went through a vast wilderness in search of Him, and now, here I am, a child of His kingdom."

"Trapped in a city of darkness." A sad smile appeared in the daughter of enmity's face as she shook her head. "You might yet find a way out of this city without returning to where you came from, sojourner, but I'm afraid it is too late for me."

The heart of the warrior princess sank at those words.

The slither turned into a snicker. <u>You know not what is coming against you, princess. She has accepted her lot, and mark my words: you will learn to accept yours.</u>

Manna

VERSES FOR MEDITATION

EVE — CURSED: *When the woman saw that the fruit of the tree was good for food and pleasing to the eye, and also desirable for gaining wisdom, she took some and ate it. She also gave some to her husband, who was with her, and he ate it.*
Genesis 3:6

"Even now," declares the Lord,
"return to me with all your heart,
with fasting and weeping and mourning."
Rend your heart
and not your garments.
Return to the Lord your God,
for he is gracious and compassionate,
slow to anger and abounding in love,
and he relents from sending calamity.
Joel 2:12-13

But if from there you seek the Lord your God, you will find him if you seek him with all your heart and with all your soul.
Deuteronomy 4:29

AUTHOR'S REFLECTIONS

It's not too late! As long as we are alive, as long as we are breathing, as long as we walk this earth, we have hope in a God Who saves, a God Who has ransomed us and redeemed us from certain death!

Is there anyone in your life, anyone you know, who once knew God, who once walked in His ways, but eventually fell away and is now following the world's ways? List down the names and pray for them. Ask God to reveal to you how to contend for their salvation. No matter how far gone they seem to be, God is a Restorer. There is yet hope for them. Let's not give up in interceding for the prodigals to find their way back home and into the Father's arms.

THE SHAMED

Righteous indignation simmered within the warrior princess at the darkening of the daughter of enmity's face. Their host pulled her cloak around her like it was some form of protection she could use to ward off their adversary's lies. How could they convince her of the hope that could anchor her soul and keep her in the kingdom of light, if only she would let it?

"Come with us." The iron maiden spoke the words the warrior princess yearned to say. "We will find a way out of this city and into the kingdom of light. They will welcome you there, I am certain of it."

"The prince will never let me out of this city. Even if you get as far as the abyss separating this city from the kingdom of light, there is no way the guards will let you pass with me in tow. I am a child of shame. The only way I can get out of here is if the King Himself storms in and takes me."

"What if we were sent here for this very purpose?" The warrior princess clung to the daughter of enmity's hand. "To seek and save the lost?"

The sentinel cleared his throat and cast a sharp glare at the warrior princess. "Perhaps we should discuss this further once we've all eaten and have rested for the night."

The daughter of enmity seemed relieved by the sentinel's interruption, so the warrior princess let go of her hand and tried to nourish herself with the meal in front of her. As she ate, she asked her Beloved if they should take their host with them. His silence was deafening. Could the winds even carry His voice to a place like this?

When dinner was over and their wards had settled in for the night, the warrior princess, the sentinel, and the iron maiden discussed at the dining table while their host cleaned up after dinner.

"Our mission is to take the blind and the deaf to the kingdom of light," the sentinel said. "She is neither blind nor deaf. Why would you ask her to join us? This is not what we have been ordered to do."

"She is desolate and full of remorse over her betrayal of the King." The iron maiden huffed. "Why shouldn't we help her if we can?"

"Because that is not for us to do." The sentinel said the words in an intense whisper, full of conviction. "That is not our mission. We can't save everyone. Especially when we don't know what lies ahead of us."

"The King's heart and purpose is to be as peace, to destroy the dividing wall of hostility between peoples," the iron maiden said. "Why should we leave one such as her amid such hostility?"

"Because that's where she chooses to be." The warrior princess sighed. "Let us rest for the night. When we awaken and she decides to go with us, then we forge ahead on this journey with her. If she chooses to stay, we will not force her. We continue on our mission, regardless."

To the warrior princess's relief, both the sentinel and the iron maiden relented.

As the warrior princess lay her head to rest, she shed a tear for the daughter of enmity. This being remained cloaked in darkness sitting in her shame when, if she would only return to Him, she would surely receive the King's amnesty.

Something about the daughter of enmity spoke to the core of the warrior princess, as if their newfound acquaintance was somehow a part of her. Perhaps it was because in a lot of ways, in a life she had left far behind, the warrior princess had once been a daughter of enmity.

Manna

Verses for Meditation

EVE — CURSED: *Then the eyes of both of them were opened, and they realized they were naked; so they sewed fig leaves together and made coverings for themselves.*
Genesis 3:7

For he himself is our peace, who has made the two groups one and has destroyed the barrier, the dividing wall of hostility, by setting aside in his flesh the law with its commands and regulations.
Ephesians 2:14

For the Son of Man came to seek and to save the lost.
Luke 19:10

We have this as a sure and steadfast anchor of the soul, a hope that enters into the inner place behind the curtain, where Jesus has gone as a forerunner on our behalf...
Hebrews 6:19-20a (ESV)

Author's Reflections

Our God is a God of reconciliation. Just as He came to destroy the dividing line between Jews and Gentiles, He can reconcile not only us to Him, but us with one another.

It's amazing how as we become more globalized, we seem to get more divided. The left and the right, the conservatives and the progressives, the rich and the poor. Race, gender, and ideologies separate us. So many hold on to whatever ground they are clinging to, yet many — though they would never admit it — are lost.

For us Christians, it is in His presence where we find our hope. It's on His Truth that we choose to lay the foundations of our lives. If only we can convince everyone to embrace His salvation and enter His presence!

Has your heart ever broken for someone whom you recognize as lost in life but can't seem to find a way to be reconciled to God? Say a prayer for that person today.

ACCURSED

Aloud, pained wail awakened the warrior princess from slumber. A quick scan of her surroundings revealed a dawn that had just broken through. The first signs of sunlight cast a warm glow into her bedroom. She rose from the single cot she had slept in and rushed outside after another cry of despair jolted her to her senses.

Upon reaching the living area, the warrior princess found the daughter of enmity curled up on the ground, distraught and rocking herself forward and back as she embraced her knees against her chest. The iron maiden was standing over her.

"What happened?" The sentinel, still wearing his night shift, rubbed his eyes open as he stepped out of his bedroom and stood next to the warrior princess.

The iron maiden cringed before hanging her head. Proving to still be her stubborn self, she took a deep breath before responding to their quizzical stares. "I tried to convince her to join us, to leave this place, so she can be secure and free of shame."

"She doesn't understand," their host muttered mostly to herself than to anyone else, "I am accursed. This is the way it has to be. This is my shame, the punishment for my folly. The prince has a hold on me. He won't let me go. I'm too weak to fight. This is my lot. I must accept it."

Those last two statements struck a cord with the warrior princess as she recognized in it the slither's lies. She knelt beside the desolate woman and stroked her forehead. "That's not true. This doesn't have to be how things are. Your prince is a prince of lies. Why do you listen to him when he has proved himself unworthy of your allegiance?"

"I can't help it. It's my curse. It's my punishment."

The iron maiden hung her shoulders in defeat. She shook her head. "It's no use reasoning with her. She believes a curse has been placed upon her, and she is tied to this city. There is no escape for her. I've told her our King has promised to set captives free, but she has convinced herself He will do nothing for her because of her betrayal of Him."

The warrior princess sighed and laid a gentle hand on the desolate woman's shoulder. She recognized in her someone not yet willing nor ready to move forward from her place of despair. She shut her eyes and waited for a peace from the One she would follow anywhere — even to a city such as this.

His conviction came over her, and though the air did not carry with it His Voice, the periods she had spent in the wilderness and in the kingdom with people of Wisdom gave the warrior princess the direction she needed. It was time to let go and move on.

In the silence, their host calmed down. It didn't take long for her to rise from where she had crumbled and prepare a meal for them, so they could be ready to move deeper into the territories of darkness.

They entertained no further talk of her joining them, and they blessed her as they went. All the while, they prayed that should the hostility against her continue, it would drive her right back to the safety of the kingdom she had once abandoned.

For now, the warrior princess couldn't afford to keep worrying about the daughter of enmity and her curse. She yet had a mission to accomplish and a city of darkness to survive. There was no way of knowing what awaited them, but a new day was a new beginning, and the warrior princess welcomed the morning light with a heart full of gratitude and an unwavering trust in a King Whot would see them through.

Manna

VERSES FOR MEDITATION

EVE — CURSED: *And I will put enmity*
between you and the woman,
and between your offspring and hers;
he will crush your head,
and you will strike his heel."
To the woman he said,
"I will make your pains in childbearing very severe;
with painful labor you will give birth to children.
Your desire will be for your husband,
and he will rule over you."
...Adam named his wife Eve, because she would become
the mother of all the living.
Genesis 3:15-16,20

But Christ has rescued us from the curse pronounced
by the law. When he was hung on the cross, he took
upon himself the curse for our wrongdoing. For it is
written in the Scriptures, "Cursed is everyone who is
hung on a tree."
Galatians 3:13 (NLT)

AUTHOR'S REFLECTIONS

Some people would rather wallow in their misery than do something about it. They would rather stay in despondent situations than risk facing the unknown. It's unfortunate, and it's heart-breaking to witness, but the victim mindset is a rampant spirit wreaking havoc in today's world.

On the flip side, there are, of course, those who are genuinely oppressed and victimized and cannot get themselves out of the situations they are in without outside help — victims of human trafficking, for example.

In both cases, we seek God for direction on how to respond. Some battles aren't ours to fight, and it takes discernment to figure out when to fight and when to walk away. What battles surround you right now? What causes move your heart and bring you to your knees? Are there people you long to see delivered from their places of desolation? How is God directing you to respond?

day 6

An Unexpected Start

Despite the disappointment she had in her heart over the daughter of enmity's choice to stay behind, hope surged within the warrior princess's soul as their group continued their journey into the unknown. Having left the daughter of enmity's ramshackle dwelling, they proceeded on their journey north, where the kingdom's capital was.

They had just passed by a busy avenue when a man with dark red wings hovered over them. His massive wings caused him to glide in the air as he backed into the direction they were heading. "What a strange sight!" he exclaimed. "You are not from here, are you?"

The warrior princess squinted her eyes against the sun's light, grateful when the stranger covered the sun's rays with his mighty wings. "We're only passing through," she said. "We want no trouble."

"I know someone you may want to take with you. Word has been going around about your presence. This is a city with a lot of secrets, but those secrets often get passed around like nothing. Word about you is you're here to seek the blind and the deaf. I know someone who's blind, and he can't wait to get out of here. Would you like to take him?"

The sentinel narrowed his eyes in suspicion. "Of course. Bring him to us."

The winged figure crossed his arms over his chest. "Not until I speak with your leader."

Everyone's eyes drifted toward the warrior princess. "That would be me," she said.

The stranger's brow rose. "You." He stroked his chin before he shrugged. "Very well then. I can't bring him to you, but I can take you to him."

Before anyone could respond, the winged creature swooped down, scooped the warrior princess up in his arms, and yelled at her gawking companions, "I'll return them to you once the fight is over!"

"Fight?" The warrior princess clung to the stranger's neck as they rose in the air. "What do you mean fight?!"

"This is a city of darkness, daughter of the day. You can't expect to get something without giving something in return."

"I have nothing to give you."

The winged stranger laughed. "Oh, but you do. Your reputation precedes you. You once conquered an army in the wilderness to get to your Beloved's kingdom. You have the favor of the King. Many will pay to see you fight. If you win, you get to take my blind captive with you. If you lose, well, you still get to take him — assuming you're still alive, that is."

His laughter echoed in the air as he took her higher and higher until the bright sunlight blinded her. This journey through enemy territory wasn't off to a promising start.

Manna

VERSES FOR MEDITATION

TAMAR — BETRAYED: *Judah got a wife for Er, his firstborn, and her name was Tamar.*
Genesis 38:6

God, make a fresh start in me, shape a Genesis week from the chaos of my life. Don't throw me out with the trash, or fail to breathe holiness in me. Bring me back from gray exile, put a fresh wind in my sails! Give me a job teaching rebels your ways so the lost can find their way home.
Psalm 51:10-13 (MSG)

AUTHOR'S REFLECTIONS

There's something about beginnings that is hopeful. New days give us a fresh start. A clean slate makes us feel like we get a new chance at something after having learned from the mistakes of the past.

However, not all beginnings turn out great. Sometimes, we feel like we are starting at a disadvantage, where others have a leg up on us. In an imperfect world such as ours, we don't always have the same opportunities and resources others may have. If we are coming from a place of failure and disappointment, new beginnings can seem daunting and scary. Sometimes, the voice of the enemy is ringing in our heads, reminding us of all the reasons we have already failed before we even start.

Whichever way we begin, however, what matters is our hearts and our willingness to obey where God is leading us. Is there a new beginning in your life that is challenging you? How are you responding? Are you eager to leap into it or are you crippled by apprehension? May God shape in you the correct heart response to this new situation!

THE FIRST STRIKE

A rush of panic swept over the warrior princess as she lay helpless in the arms of this stranger who was carrying her into the unknown. They couldn't have taken flight longer than a few minutes, but it felt to her as if days had already passed since this winged creature had forced her to leave her group, so she could be their source of entertainment in some sort of fight.

"Stop squirming," he said. "You don't want me to drop you."

Uncomfortable, she wriggled herself in his arms, trying to get into a more comfortable position. Annoyed, the winged one tossed her in the open air, and she dropped into a free fall.

How had this happened? Where were the King and His subjects? Was no one coming to save her?

She shut her eyes and whispered, "Save me," refusing to believe this would be her end.

Suddenly, brawny arms caught her and scooped her back up. When she scrambled to find out who had saved her, it was, to her dismay, the very stranger who had dropped her in the first place.

She would have yelled at him and demanded an explanation, but her heart was racing too fast, and her entire system was grasping for calm. She couldn't believe how she was at the mercy of this callous stranger, who was snickering at her.

"Behave and do as I tell you, and you'll get to your destination safely." He shook his head as he tsk-tsked. "You're making it hard for me to believe the stories about you. The rumors paint you as a frightening warrior, formidable in battle, yet here you are. Frail and frightened in my arms."

While everything in her wanted to defend herself from this fool's perception of her, she held her tongue. Something told her an argument with him over her experience in battle was not a fight she needed to get into. Besides, it wasn't her who had won her battles, but the Spirit of her Beloved fighting alongside her, with her, for her.

She summoned peace within and told herself to not fear the predicament she was in and to not be too irked by this fool who had taken her captive.

"Here we are!" he announced after a few minutes of flight.

The warrior princess dared glance at what was beneath her, and at their descent, she found the clouds parting to reveal a large pit carved deep into the ground.

At the shock in her eyes, her captor laughed. "I have to leave you here for a moment to prepare for the fight. Worry not, warrior. I will return soon."

Once they hovered right at the top of the pit, the winged creature dropped her. The fall was a few feet down — enough to bruise her but not break her. It took a few gasps of breath for her to gather her wits about her as she groaned at the unexpected fall. She scanned her surroundings and discovered one lone figure in the pit with her.

A blind man.

Her heart leaped at the sight of him even as a warmth enveloped her. This unexpected predicament yet had a purpose, for their mission was to bring the blind and the deaf to the King's capital, and here was one of them, waiting to get delivered. If only someone would deliver the warrior princess as well.

Manna

Verses for Meditation

Tamar — Betrayed: *But Er, Judah's firstborn, was wicked in the Lord's sight; so the Lord put him to death.*
Genesis 38:7

The Lord will fight for you; you need only to be still.
Exodus 14:14

You will not have to fight this battle. Take up your positions; stand firm and see the deliverance the Lord will give you, Judah and Jerusalem. Do not be afraid; do not be discouraged. Go out to face them tomorrow, and the Lord will be with you.
2 Chronicles 20:17

Author's Reflections

Genesis tells the story of Tamar, who was married off to one of Judah's sons, Er. Nothing much was said about her marriage or her husband other than he was wicked, so the Lord put him to death. We can only imagine what her life was like with one who was so wicked, the Lord Himself struck him down. It's perhaps safe to say it wasn't a happy marriage.

When placed in situations where we feel helpless and hopeless, where we can't control our surroundings and we are left feeling stuck, how do we respond? Are we able to calm down and trust God to see us through, no matter how hopeless and dire the situation seems? Has there been cases in the past where you were caught between a rock and a hard place, but God saw you through, and so, here you are, still standing? Take a moment to reflect and thank Him for those moments. If you are in such a moment right now, pray over the situation, be still, and let God be God over your life.

THE SECOND STRIKE

Attuned to the slightest of movements and sounds around him, the blind man yanked his head to the side, facing the warrior princess, who was still groaning from her fall. "Who's there?" he asked. "Did I hear the flap of he whose wings are the shade of blood?"

"You did," the warrior princess replied. "He was the one who threw me in here with you. What an insufferable miscreant!"

The blind man chuckled. "Sounds like him, all right. Are you who he says you are? The woman whose heart follows hard after the King of Light?"

"He told you about me?"

The blind man nodded.

"Did he tell you about this fight he wants me to engage in?"

"So that's what he wants from you. I wondered about his insistence on finding you and bringing you here."

"He says you want to join us in our quest to get out of this city and to the capital of the kingdom of light. Is that true?"

"Yes. I no longer want to remain his captive, at the mercy of his unpredictable whims. I want to be free."

The warrior princess gave the blind captive a resolute nod. Even if he couldn't see her determination, she hoped he would detect it in her voice. "Free, you shall be, because

I have come on behalf of a King Whose rule sets captives free."

At that, the blind man scoffed. "Ha! How can you be so naïve? Have you been listening to fairy tales? Such a king doesn't exist. If he does, then why allow a city like this to thrive? We are in a city of traitors, where even those you trust most, those who should look out for you are the very ones who will end up destroying you. You must be new to these parts, warrior, because the further you go into this city, the darker, more cutthroat things will prove to be. Think my brother is a miscreant? You've seen nothing yet."

Her head spun. Brother?

"What lies are you now spinning against me, brother?"

The warrior princess's gaze shot up to find her captor standing by the edge of the pit, his arms crossed over his chest, his wings spread wide behind him. Her fellow captive turned toward the sound of their captor's voice. Only then did she notice the broken wings on his back.

What betrayal had this man suffered and had it been a blow dealt to him by his own brother?

Manna

VERSES FOR MEDITATION

TAMAR — BETRAYED: *Then Judah said to Onan, "Sleep with your brother's wife and fulfill your duty to her as a brother-in-law to raise up offspring for your brother." But Onan knew that the child would not be his; so whenever he slept with his brother's wife, he spilled his semen on the ground to keep from providing offspring for his brother. What he did was wicked in the Lord's sight; so the Lord put him to death also.*
Genesis 38:8-10

*The Spirit of the Sovereign Lord is on me,
because the Lord has anointed me
to proclaim good news to the poor.
He has sent me to bind up the brokenhearted,
to proclaim freedom for the captives
and release from darkness for the prisoners*
Isaiah 61:1

AUTHOR'S REFLECTIONS

Have you experienced the agony of betrayal? It's one thing to be hurt by strangers or by foes; it's quite another thing to experience hurt from people close to us, people we cherish, people we treasure as our own. In a world lauding the survival of the fittest, what place is there for the broken? For the captives? For the prisoners?

We are surrounded by people who have once held on to hopes and dreams for their future, only to encounter deception and betrayal at the hands of people they love. If you've experienced something like that, you know how painful it is.

And yet, this is the very reason Jesus came. To proclaim good news, to heal, to set free. Is there someone who needs to be set free in your life? Is it you? Whoever it is, say a prayer for that person now.

THE FINAL BLOW

Indignation simmered inside the warrior princess's chest. What were these games their captor was playing? What did he want?

"You said you wanted to fight in exchange for our freedom!" she yelled. "Let's fight now. You and me!"

A grin spread across the face of their captor. "You? Fight me?"

"Woman, this is foolish." The blind captive shook his head, his empty gaze darting in random directions. "He is a seasoned warrior."

"So am I," she said.

"Not the same way he is."

"How would you know?"

"You are in this pit, and he isn't."

"Listen to him, princess." Their captor snickered. "I must admit, it's nice to see some fight in you. What was it? An hour ago? You were quivering in my arms, begging for mercy."

"No such thing happened." Rage was building up inside her as the warrior princess tightened her jaw. It was at that moment she recognized she was no longer acting from a place of peace and trust in the One Who had sent her there. Her hope wasn't in her own strength or ability to fight anyone, but in Whom she served. She took a deep breath and cleared her throat. "Are you the one who did this to your brother? Took away his sight? Prevented him from free flight?"

"Is that what this fool told you?"

"It's true!" The blind captive stomped his foot on the dusty ground. His lip twitched.

The warrior princess sensed she wasn't being given the complete truth. What was she to do now? Did it matter which of the two was telling the truth? What was important was for her to get back to her group and to bring the blind captive with her if he would so choose. "If I win a fight with your brother, will you come to the kingdom of light with me?"

"Will I be captive there?"

"You will be free, but you will need to live by the laws of our kingdom if you wish to stay."

"If I choose to leave and return to this city?"

"No one will stop you."

"I will go."

The warrior princess directed her glare at her captor. "Do you promise to let us go if I win this fight against you?"

"You have my word you and my brother will have your freedom if you win, but I said nothing about the fight being against me, princess."

"Who is it against then?"

Their winged captor smirked and snapped his fingers, and in the blink of an eye, they were in the middle of a large, round arena. Beyond the deafening yells of the bloodthirsty crowd filling the amphitheater, a familiar sound caught her attention. The flap of the scaled wings of a mighty dragon.

Her breath caught in her chest as she raised her eyes upward to find a familiar foe looming over her, blocking the sun from shining its light on her.

Her captor threw a shield and a sword at her feet. "Win, warrior princess," he said, "and alongside my brother, I myself will go to the kingdom of light with you."

The warrior princess locked gazes with him and caught the flicker of desperation in his eyes. Was he a captive of the darkness, as well?

She picked up her shield and her sword and tried to ignore the fear sweeping over her. It took over like it had so many times when she had still been in the wilderness, but this time, a soft breeze caressed her skin, and with the wind, came her Beloved's kind, but urgent, words.

Be strong and courageous...

She smiled, knowing she wasn't about to fight this battle alone.

Manna

VERSES FOR MEDITATION

TAMAR — BETRAYED: *Judah then said to his daughter-in-law Tamar, "Live as a widow in your father's household until my son Shelah grows up." For he thought, "He may die too, just like his brothers." So Tamar went to live in her father's household.*
Genesis 38:11

'Not by might nor by power, but by my Spirit,' says the Lord Almighty.
Zechariah 4:6b

Have I not commanded you? Be strong and courageous. Do not be afraid; do not be discouraged, for the Lord your God will be with you wherever you go.
Joshua 1:9

AUTHOR'S REFLECTIONS

There are seasons in life when we encounter wave upon wave of opposition. Just when we feel confident we have what it takes to overcome one obstacle, yet another one comes up. Sometimes, the enemy attacks us with a strategy of relentless attrition, throwing at us one blow after another, one obstacle after another, one giant after another.

Attrition is defined as *the action or process of gradually reducing the strength or effectiveness of someone or something through sustained attack or pressure.* We must recognize this strategy and learn how to come against it or stand our ground amid all the attacks, because if our strength is coming not from us but from the Lord, we will prevail.

How?

Remember the enemy can only go on for so long. Patience is a fruit of the Spirit, something the enemy doesn't have.

THE CONTENDER

She had already been in a situation like this before. It was in a different setting, but it was the same exact thing. In the wilderness, the odds had been stacked against her, but she kept on fighting anyway, and she had prevailed. She had already won over this adversary before. The stunning realization swept over the warrior princess as she stood — a lone figure — in the middle of an arena of strangers crying out for violence. The winged brothers who had brought her there had gone off to the sides, presumably hoping for her victory.

Her grip on her weapons tightened as she looked up at her foe. How she was going to fight a dragon, she didn't know, but she knew her mission, her heritage, and her destiny. This was a fight she wasn't about to back out on.

The dragon swooped down and breathed fire on her. She raised her shield to protect herself, casting out any doubt the small shield of iron would be able to protect her. It wasn't, after all, her weapons that would sustain her, but her King. To her amazement and delight, the shield didn't melt under the heat, nor did she sense the blaze of the dragon's fiery breath at all. Like a force field, the King's favor surrounded her.

As she stood her ground, a desperate-sounding slither wormed into her ear. <u>Why would He show you favor when you were too weak to protect your own people? Here you</u>

are in a fight not of your own choosing, while the people you are to rescue have been left abandoned. Do you even know where the sentinel, the iron maiden, and the kingdom's children are?

The warrior princess laughed. She didn't need to respond, because the slither already knew the answer to that. They may be behind enemy lines, but they were still under the protection of the King. Neither the prince of darkness nor the slither nor the dragon can do them actual harm. The only harm and danger that could come against them were the ones they allowed.

The warrior princess lowered her shield and stood in the middle of a dragon's firestorm, unscathed. She reveled in the victory and power of the King to Whom she had given her allegiance to. Though she couldn't see, she could tell He was right there with her.

The dragon's breath finally ran out. The warrior princess's smile grew as she clung to the hilt of the sword, aimed, and launched it upwards toward her target; the sword cut through the already-exhausted dragon's left wing. It screeched in pain before flying away from a fight that would only tire the creature and renew her strength.

The crowd yelled as the dragon flew away, wounded and defeated. She dropped her weapons on the ground. Her captor and the blind captive approached. Though it still irked her to see the winged one, she couldn't deny him passage to the kingdom of light if he asked for it, so the one whom she earlier considered a foe was now her traveling companion.

Such was the way of following her King. So, through strange contention between two brothers, broken wings, and dragon's breath, her victory added two to their band of sojourners, traveling from darkness into light.

Manna

Verses for Meditation

Tamar — Betrayed: *As she was being brought out, she sent a message to her father-in-law. "I am pregnant by the man who owns these," she said. And she added, "See if you recognize whose seal and cord and staff these are." Judah recognized them and said, "She is more righteous than I, since I wouldn't give her to my son Shelah." And he did not sleep with her again.*
Genesis 38:25-26

*no weapon forged against you will prevail,
and you will refute every tongue that accuses you.
This is the heritage of the servants of the Lord,
and this is their vindication from me,"
declares the Lord.*
Isaiah 54:17

*Surely, Lord, you bless the righteous;
you surround them with your favor as with a shield.*
Psalm 5:12

Author's Reflections

More often than not, the enemy's attempts to derail us are mostly bark, no bite. As children of light, ransomed by the blood of the Lamb, the enemy doesn't hold any true power over us — not unless we give him a foothold in our lives.

That means our destiny is ours for the taking.

In the story of Tamar, she had suffered one injustice after another, and if it were up to the people in her lives, if it were up to the enemy, she would have been denied her rightful inheritance. She did something daring and unexpected for a woman of her time, and Judah declared her more righteous than he. The Messiah will eventually be born from her heritage, and she wouldn't have had the honor of being one of the few women named as an ancestor of Christ had she not stood her ground and ignored the enemy's attempts to destroy her or steal her inheritance from her.

How is the enemy trying to throw you off and steal away what is rightfully given to you by God? How can you contend for your inheritance?

day 11

A Cry for Help

They were free to go, but they yet faced one obstacle before them. Her captor — now fellow traveler — had wings strong enough to only carry one passenger in flight. His blind brother's wings were still broken. Meanwhile, the warrior princess was still bristling at the thought of traveling anywhere with her two companions. Neither inspired great trust in her, but if they were willing to join her on her journey, she wouldn't be the one to stop them. After all, her King knew better than her in these matters. She could trust Him to sort them out Himself.

"What do we do now?" the brother asked. "I can't carry you both."

The warrior princess circled the blind man and assessed his broken wings. "What broke his wings to begin with?"

"He broke it!" The blind one pointed at his brother.

"It was an accident! It happens to all of us. We fall, and we break. We always eventually heal, but he didn't. I don't know why."

A sense of urgency captured the warrior princess. It had been hours since the winged one had taken her from her group. She had no idea where to even find them at this point. Had they stayed where she had been taken or had they the good sense to continue on with the journey without her, trusting the King would find a way to return her to them?

What was she to do now? She stared at the blind man with broken wings. She couldn't leave him behind, this she knew for sure. Right then, a recollection from the depths of her heart surfaced — her Beloved's words written to remind her of the power of hope. She recalled the despair in the blind man's words when they were yet at the pit.

"My friend—" she laid a hand on his broken wings "— you have been broken and you stay broken, because you've lost hope in the possibility of getting fixed. Yet, I am here to tell you we are in this city of darkness specifically to bring all the blind and the deaf to our good King's territories. Don't you see? There is yet hope for you! What if the only reason we had to go through this city was to find you? That's how precious you are to the King. Take heart! Have hope! It will renew your strength."

As she had spoken each word, the blind man's countenance had changed and lightened. By the time she finished speaking, his wings spread across his back.

Finally! Delight swept over the warrior princess as the brothers swept her up in the air, ready to return to her people. Her relief, however, was short-lived, because not long after they had taken flight, a scene in a tower they were about to pass gave them pause.

From a window sill, a scarlet garment waved like a flag drawing attention. A familiar figure appeared from the window and cried out, "Help!"

Manna

VERSES FOR MEDITATION

RAHAB — DESPERATE: *Then Joshua son of Nun secretly sent two spies from Shittim. "Go, look over the land," he said, "especially Jericho." So they went and entered the house of a prostitute named Rahab and stayed there.*
Joshua 2:1

May the God of hope fill you with all joy and peace as you trust in him, so that you may overflow with hope by the power of the Holy Spirit.
Romans 15:13

*but those who hope in the Lord
will renew their strength.
They will soar on wings like eagles;
they will run and not grow weary,
they will walk and not be faint.*
Isaiah 40:31

AUTHOR'S REFLECTIONS

Hope. We serve a God in Whom we can hope, and in the world we live in, amid war and pestilence, amid disease and death, it is far too easy to lose hope. So many people entered the year 2020 with so much hope and anticipation for the future, believing it would be a great year, a different year. No one expected a pandemic to hit and put the world on pause. For months, the world stood still. Entire countries went on lockdown. So many people lost hope and ended their lives. A quick search on the internet will confirm an increase in suicide rates during the pandemic.

Countless found themselves depressed or divorced, many searching for answers.

As Christians, how do we respond to these things? Were we ourselves hit by depression and a lack of hope? Or were we the ones who became a source of hope for others? We cannot lose our hope. We need to stay connected to the God Who anchors our souls.

As the times grow darker, this is truer than ever before. Hold on to hope. Fight for it. Share it with the world, because in this day and age, everyone could use some hope.

A Favor Given

At the warrior princess's insistence on stopping and responding to the woman's cry for help, the winged brothers resisted.

"We don't have time!" The strong brother said. "We must find your people and get to the kingdom of light before nightfall."

"Why?" The warrior princess frowned. "We can find a place to rest for the night if we need to. Besides, I know her. She is the daughter of enmity, I'm sure of it."

"You don't understand!" The winged one shook his head. "She is known around these parts as the scarlet woman. It is better not to meddle with one like her. Especially as we are about to pass through the heart of the city. We are better off without her."

"No." The warrior princess shifted herself in the arms of the strong one to get a better view of the scarlet woman crying out for help. "We cannot abandon her, especially when she's asking for help! It's not the way of the kingdom!"

"You are not in the kingdom, princess!" The strong one tightened his hold on her. "It's not how things are done in this city. Many need help around here. You can't stop for everyone who asks for it. Especially one such as her."

"I may not be in the kingdom, but I am of the kingdom. We will help her!"

The strong brother grunted. "Fine." He then instructed his blind brother to stay where he was before changing course and returning to the tower where the daughter of enmity was. He set the warrior princess on the gabled roof to approach her friend.

The frantic look in the woman's eyes made the warrior princess's heart ache. Why was she so afraid? She seemed calm when they had left her earlier. This time, there was a desperation about her that told the warrior princess far more than what was being said.

"What happened?" the warrior princess asked. "Why are you here?"

"Please take me with you. I need to get out of this city before they discover what I've done!"

"What have you done?"

The scarlet woman's silence spoke volumes. The warrior princess looked at her winged carrier. "We have to take her with us."

"Why?" The winged one was incredulous. "We don't even know what she did! What if she's a fugitive?"

"She's helped us before, and she wants to go with me. That's all I need to know."

The winged one narrowed his eyes. "I'm warning you. The greater our number, the more difficult it is for us to get through this city unharmed."

The warrior princess shrugged. "It's a good thing we don't operate in the ways of the city. It is the King's ways we will follow, and that's the only way we'll get through."

So, they yet added to their crew another sojourner — the scarlet woman, a daughter of enmity, with desperate eyes being carried into the unknown by a blind winged sojourner.

Manna

VERSES FOR MEDITATION

RAHAB — DESPERATE: *So the king of Jericho sent this message to Rahab: "Bring out the men who came to you and entered your house, because they have come to spy out the whole land." But the woman had taken the two men and hidden them.*
Joshua 2:3-4

So here's what I want you to do, God helping you: Take your everyday, ordinary life—your sleeping, eating, going-to-work, and walking-around life—and place it before God as an offering. Embracing what God does for you is the best thing you can do for him. Don't become so well-adjusted to your culture that you fit into it without even thinking. Instead, fix your attention on God. You'll be changed from the inside out. Readily recognize what he wants from you, and quickly respond to it. Unlike the culture around you, always dragging you down to its level of immaturity, God brings the best out of you, develops well-formed maturity in you.
Romans 12:1-2 (MSG)

AUTHOR'S REFLECTIONS

It's easy to watch how the world works nowadays and make our decisions according to how things operate around us, according to the world's patterns and systems. We, however, are kingdom people who are ambassadors of the kingdom of God. We are to bring His kingdom culture — not our own — wherever we go. (This, of course, doesn't refer to earthly cultures, with us imposing our native culture on the cultures of the people we are trying to reach.)

It's kingdom culture we are after — a kingdom where we are to love our enemies, where we are taught to be meek, to put others before ourselves, to be poor in spirit. We belong to a kingdom where to be the greatest is to be a servant to all, a kingdom where the last becomes the first, and the first becomes the last. It's that kingdom culture we are furthering, and one glimpse at the world around us tells us kingdom culture is counter-culture to what the world propagates.

How are you representing kingdom culture in your life right now?

The Promise & the Condition

A sigh of relief escaped the warrior princess's lips when they reached a small clearing at the center of a busy intersection, where her band of travelers were waiting. When the quartet arrived, her squad was standing in a circle, hands clasped together, eyes closed.

When the sentinel opened his eyes and saw the warrior princess, relief crossed his face. "You're safe! We have been interceding on your behalf!"

The entire group gathered around her and waited for their turn to embrace their leader.

"We thought we had lost you," the iron maiden said.

"I assumed you would have continued on your journey, anyway," the warrior princess replied. "You must accomplish the mission with or without me, after all."

The sentinel shook his head. "We couldn't. A friend of yours came to both warn us and assure us."

"A friend?" the warrior princess asked.

The iron maiden sighed. "Flighty little winged woman who calls herself Faith, but says you know her as Folly from the wilderness."

Surprise washed over the warrior princess. "She was here? Where is she now?"

"She left after giving us her message, saying she will look for you when the time is right."

That comforted the warrior princess. "I hope to see her again soon, but what was her message?"

The sentinel nodded. "The warning is we cannot go through the gates unless we are complete." His wary eyes scanned the warrior princess's companions; his focus darted particularly between the red-winged warrior who had taken the warrior princess and the scarlet woman, whom he yet knew as the daughter of enmity. "She also said we must be discerning, because even friends can prove to be foe in a city such as this."

The warrior princess tried to grasp the meaning behind his words, but set aside the lingering unsettledness for other matters. "What is the assurance?"

"She says the King has given assurance we need only be still, and you will be returned to us. The King will keep you safe—" the iron maiden smiled "—and here you now are with us!"

"She also gave us a promise and a condition," the sentinel added.

"What is it?" the warrior princess asked.

"The day of this city's destruction is drawing near. We will be safe through it all, but we must first ascertain who is the criminal among us." A sternness made the sentinel's face tense up. "We cannot enter the kingdom of light with blood on our hands."

Immediately, all eyes traveled to the winged one who had been her captor.

He smirked. "Of course you would blame me," he said. "Believe it or not, however, I'm no criminal. My hands are not stained by blood. In fact, isn't it she—" he pointed at the warrior princess "—who has a reputation for slaughtering soldiers in battle?"

The warrior princess's inner defenses threatened to rise up, but nightfall was coming and they were about to enter the heart of the city. This could wait. "Let's continue on. We can sort this out later. For now, we keep moving."

And so they did, but an uneasy distrust simmered between the original ten and the recent addition of three. It grieved the heart of the warrior princess, because deep down, she knew they wouldn't be able to survive this journey unless they found a way towards unity.

Manna

Verses for Meditation

Rahab — Desperate: *"Our lives for your lives!" the men assured her. "If you don't tell what we are doing, we will treat you kindly and faithfully when the Lord gives us the land."*
Joshua 2:14

But avoid foolish controversies and genealogies and arguments and quarrels about the law, because these are unprofitable and useless.
Titus 3:9

I appeal to you, brothers and sisters, in the name of our Lord Jesus Christ, that all of you agree with one another in what you say and that there be no divisions among you, but that you be perfectly united in mind and thought.
1 Corinthians 1:10

Author's Reflections

There is something about being out in the fields of harvest that unites Christians. Our focus becomes fixed on the harvest rather than the shortcomings of one another. This is even truer of the church in persecuted nations, where to find a fellow Christian who shares one's heart is in itself balm to the soul. It is usually in comfortable Christian nations where we have time to squabble over doctrines and the fine print of Scripture. In the harvest fields, where the workers are few, most Christians are just happy to be able to fellowship with one another.

Still, as proved by the Christians of the early church — most of which were experiencing persecution —

there can still be dissension within the churches of the persecuted. A lot of it comes from a genuine desire to guard the Truth, especially since we are warned that in the last days, there will be great deception. We need to be vigilant and recognize there are tares among the wheat, but we must also be careful that this vigilance not turn into a religious or critical spirit fostered by an unhealthy distrust of fellow followers of Christ. We all are works in progress, after all, and God sees our hearts. Let us allow Him to sort us all out — which ones are His and which ones are not. Meanwhile, let us focus on the task He has given us and make sure we accomplish it!

day 14

A Precarious Situation

As they walked on, the scarlet woman trailed behind the rest of their group. A mixture of suspicion, empathy, and curiosity filled the warrior princess for the daughter of enmity. What had made her change her mind and join them? Why had she been so desperate to leave the tower? Was she the criminal they had to identify? The warrior princess nudged the sentinel to join her in trying to converse with the woman and hopefully get her to be more comfortable with them.

"I'm glad you decided to come," the sentinel said as they both walked alongside their new fellow sojourner. "However, something seems to be bothering you."

The scarlet woman bowed her head. "I've already told you what I did to betray your King. What I didn't tell you is I am an unclean woman. I'm afraid one like me will have no place in a kingdom of light, but I am at a point of desperation. This city will be my ruin if I stay behind."

The warrior princess and the sentinel exchanged sympathetic glances, though the way the sentinel flinched at the woman's mention of her uncleanness had not escaped the warrior princess's eye.

"They will be after me."

"Who will be after you?" the warrior princess asked.

"The ones who believe I belong to them. It may be so, for they purchased me as a slave a long time ago. It's why I believe I am tied to this city. I fear I might only be a hindrance to your mission if I stay with you."

"What happened?" the warrior princess asked. "Why did you cry out to us for help?"

"It's me." The scarlet woman raised her hands midair, palms up. "I am the criminal, the one with blood on her hands, the one who might prevent you from entering His kingdom. I am a woman marked for destruction. Your King's mercy is my last thread of hope for survival, because the hostility against me in this city has grown to the point of life-threatening."

"What have you done?" the sentinel asked.

The scarlet woman took a deep breath. "After you left my apartment, I went to the tower where I work for those who claim ownership of me. I arrived to find one of our handlers beating up my friend — a daughter of enmity like me. I—" she bit her lip "—tried to help her."

"How did you do that?" The sentinel's questions became more urgent. "Did you kill him?"

The warrior princess glared at him, but the question had slipped out of his mouth and could no longer be taken back. Her heart fell when the scarlet woman nodded.

"We can't go on with her." The sentinel shook her head. "Faith said—"

"She said we need to ascertain who the criminal is. Now we know. Faith also said we can't get past the gates unless we are complete."

"Nor can we enter the kingdom of light with blood in our hands."

All three exchanged uncertain looks, for they have found themselves in quite the precarious situation.

Manna

Verses for Meditation

RAHAB — DESPERATE: *So the young men who had done the spying went in and brought out Rahab, her father and mother, her brothers and sisters and all who belonged to her. They brought out her entire family and put them in a place outside the camp of Israel.*
Joshua 6:23

Jesus answered them, "It is not the healthy who need a doctor, but the sick. I have not come to call the righteous, but sinners to repentance."
Luke 5:31-32

For the creation was subjected to frustration, not by its own choice, but by the will of the one who subjected it, in hope that the creation itself will be liberated from its bondage to decay and brought into the freedom and glory of the children of God.
Romans 8:20-21

Author's Reflections

The more we witness the darkness of the world, the more our hearts break. So many around us are victims of darkness, and we can often feel helpless in doing anything about it. So many are brutalized, ravished, destroyed by evil — and many are not even aware this is being done to them.

Poet Henry Thoreau writes, "The mass of men lead lives of quiet desperation."

This rings true even in the book of Ecclesiastes, where a wise king decries the meaninglessness of life under the sun.

And yet, in Christ, Who came to seek and save the lost, we have an undying hope that we can be set free. There is light in the darkness. We are light in the darkness. We live in desperate times, and there are many crying out for salvation. May we hear the call and respond to it, so more will be "brought into the freedom and glory of the children of God."

An Unlikely Match

A brush of wind grazed their skins. The moment it passed, the sentinel's glare toward the scarlet woman transformed from suspicion to compassion. It happened suddenly, like something had shifted within the sentinel. The sternness of his countenance shifted into a kindness that could only come from the King's inner workings within the hearts of His subjects. The warrior princess had seen it many times before during her time in the kingdom of light — and even in the wilderness — the compassion of the King manifested in the transformed lives of His followers.

"Our King is good." The sentinel laid his hand over the shoulder of the woman. "He will show us the way. I yet believe you can be a daughter of light, if you would only humble yourself before the King."

The scarlet woman's dark eyes cleared and a flicker of hope lightened her face.

At peace with the interaction, the warrior princess left the two to speak. She had other concerns to address — one of which was the looming danger they had been repeatedly warned about. She approached the only person who would have knowledge about such a matter — the seeing winged one whose scowl made it clear he wasn't having a pleasant conversation with the iron maiden walking alongside him.

"What's going on here?" the warrior princess asked.

"I think he is the criminal," the iron maiden said.

"You have no proof of that!" The winged one huffed, his face darkening as he simmered at the kingdom child walking beside him.

"Who else would it be?" the iron maiden scowled right back at him. "He's neither blind nor deaf nor a child of light. He is not who we are tasked to bring to the kingdom of light, yet he is on this journey with us for some reason. How can we trust one such as him when he clearly doesn't belong among us?"

<u>She's right. Why did you let this man join you? You are wiser than this, princess.</u>

The words rung with truth, so the woman barely recognized the slither the statement had come from, but she remembered the scarlet woman's confession. This man wasn't the criminal, and he wanted to go to the kingdom of light. None of them had any business stopping him from going. Before she could speak up for him, however, their winged companion halted. His breath hitched.

Ahead of them was a tall wall reaching in both directions — east and west — as far as their eyes could see.

"The heart of the city," the winged one said.

"What about it?" the iron maiden asked.

"That's where the prince of darkness is most powerful."

"Let's find a way around it then," the warrior princess said.

The winged one shook his head. "There is no going around it or over it. We have to go through it. Few have gone past that wall and returned."

Somehow, this sounded like a good thing to the warrior princess. She smiled. "Maybe because they managed to pass through and reach the kingdom of light."

Up for a challenge, she squared her shoulders and marched her group forward, trusting in the safe passage a King as powerful as hers could provide.

Manna

Verses for Meditation

RAHAB — DESPERATE: *But Joshua spared Rahab the prostitute, with her family and all who belonged to her, because she hid the men Joshua had sent as spies to Jericho—and she lives among the Israelites to this day.*
Joshua 6:25

There is no fear in love. But perfect love drives out fear, because fear has to do with punishment. The one who fears is not made perfect in love.
1 John 4:18

*Even though I walk through the darkest valley,
I will fear no evil, for you are with me;
your rod and your staff, they comfort me.*
Psalm 23:4

Author's Reflections

Following Jesus doesn't spare us from walking through dark valleys and encountering dangerous situations that threaten our very lives. We are born into a time of war and whether we like it or not, as Christians, we are targets for attack by the enemy. There is no going around it. Jesus even promised it to His disciples and told them to accept it. In this world, we will face trouble, but we are not dismayed, because He has overcome the world.

In this season, God is taking many of His children through a period of challenging our endurance. We need to learn to endure the troubles of this world, for even this, God can use to refine us. What are you learning to endure in this season? Are you enduring with fear you won't make it? Or with a smile, because you know He is love, and He can get you through to the other side?

The Woman of Sorrows

Upon reaching the gate leading them to the walled heart of the city of darkness, guards cloaked in black and armed with an assortment of weapons — bows and arrows, swords and daggers — immediately surrounded them.

Two women among their group became the sharp focus of these men's close surveillance: the warrior princess and the scarlet woman. A hushed and cautious silence came over everyone as the cloaked guards with hidden faces circled them.

One stopped right in front of the warrior princess. "You have amongst you a woman of the scarlet order. She has escaped from her master and must be returned immediately."

The warrior princess shook her head. "The King of the kingdom of light, of which we are ambassadors, has ransomed her. We demand safe passage through the heart of the city, so we can reach our destination."

"You demand, do you?" The guard scoffed at her. "Your King isn't king here."

"My King is king no matter where I go, and should you harm a hair on my head or hurt any of my comrades, He will find out about it. His justice and vindication will follow."

"We do not fear your king here, woman. You do not know this harlot. She does not belong to the kingdom of light. She is a child of darkness and will always be. If you discover the atrocities she has experienced and committed, you will find out how your King has abandoned her. He wants nothing to do with one such as her. She belongs in the darkest pit among the darkest of creatures, because she is a woman of sorrows, most unclean of all women, rejected and derided by all who encounter her."

The warrior princess turned around to see the scarlet woman in tears. Just by the expression on her face, the warrior princess could tell she believed all the words the guard had spoken about her. What had the scarlet woman gone through?

"Let them pass." The scarlet woman lifted her hands in surrender. "I will surrender if you give them safe passage. The sun will set soon. They still have a long way to go before they reach their destination."

The guard facing the warrior princess smirked. "See? She knows her place. Now, know yours, and realize you don't have power here. The darkness is coming soon. You best be going." He snapped his fingers and pointed at the scarlet woman. "Arrest her!"

"No!" the sentinel exclaimed, but they were outnumbered and overpowered, and the warrior princess recognized it wasn't the right time to fight. She nodded toward the sentinel to let them take the scarlet woman.

Once the guards had gone, dragging the woman of sorrows with them, the sentinel demanded an explanation from her.

"We must find a place to stay for the night," the warrior princess said. "We are not leaving the heart of this city without her."

The warrior princess had no idea how to fight this fight, but she trusted the King could come through for them. She could tell she wasn't about to get a wink of sleep that night — not until one who was rightfully theirs could be set free.

Manna

Verses for Meditation

RUTH — GRIEVED: *They married Moabite women, one named Orpah and the other Ruth. After they had lived there about ten years, both Mahlon and Kilion also died, and Naomi was left without her two sons and her husband.*
Ruth 1:4-5

For he has not despised or scorned the suffering of the afflicted one; he has not hidden his face from him but has listened to his cry for help.
Psalm 22:24

The Lord is a refuge for the oppressed, a stronghold in times of trouble.
Psalm 9:9

Author's Reflections

At some point in your life, you've probably heard someone question the existence of God, because if there is an all-powerful, kind, and loving God, why is there so much pain in the world? So much grief, sorrow, and injustice?

You may have asked these questions yourself. Why does it sometimes feel like God has abandoned us, turned His back on us? The temptation to surrender to despair — to what seems like inevitable destruction — is strong. We are tempted to run away from a God Who doesn't seem to come through for us, but the Bible says the Lord is a refuge for the oppressed. He is someone we can run to in times of trouble, not someone we run from.

When the enemy makes it seem like we have been forsaken, we press further into the presence of God. This is when we need to lean on Him — our refuge — the most! He listens. He will not reject us. Our cries for help will not fall on deaf ears. Let us believe that to be true and depend on a God Who stays with us through seasons of sorrow and grief.

day 17

THE HOPELESS FUTURE

The moment their wards had settled down and their winged companions had gone off to bed, the warrior princess, the sentinel, and the iron maiden gathered inside one room of the inn to talk about what needed to be done to spare the scarlet woman's life and deliver her out of a pit of destruction.

"We can't leave the city without her." The warrior princess stomped her foot to emphasize her point, before she continued to pace back and forth next to the bed where the iron maiden sat.

"I agree," the iron maiden said. "We can't leave even one behind if she wishes to go with us, because we serve a King who would leave ninety-nine for one."

The sentinel sat silently on a wooden bench next to the wall. He hadn't said a word since the scarlet woman had been taken. He shook his head. "We shouldn't have let them take her away." He cast an accusatory glare at their leader.

The warrior princess bristled. "We had no choice in the matter. We would have risked the safety of our other wards had we pushed the guards to relent."

"We could have saved her! Now, we won't even know where to find her or how to start!" The sentinel's voice grew louder as every word came out of his lips.

The warrior princess wondered at his rising rage. He had always been so calm and collected. "We won't be able to help her if we go against one another, sentinel. Let's come to a place of agreement before we come up with a plan, but before that, your agitation is cause for concern. What is truly irking you, my friend?"

The sentinel lowered his gaze. "I heard the King's voice. He wants her returned to His Kingdom."

The warrior princess and the iron maiden exchanged glances. A tinge of jealousy grew in the warrior princess's heart. Who was she to the King?

"Let us come together then," the warrior princess said. "We must devise a strategy to help her."

With a harrumph, the sentinel nodded. They all took a seat around a circle table to discuss what to do next, but dawn had risen, and they still weren't sure what to do.

All seemed hopeless, but if there was one thing all three of them agreed on by the time morning came, they were not about to give up hope, and that determination alone made the future nowhere near hopeless.

Manna

Verses for Meditation

RUTH — GRIEVED: *But Naomi said, "Return home, my daughters. Why would you come with me? Am I going to have any more sons, who could become your husbands? ... It is more bitter for me than for you, because the Lord's hand has turned against me!"*
Ruth 1:11,13b

*I waited patiently for the Lord;
he turned to me and heard my cry.*
Psalm 40:1

Though one may be overpowered, two can defend themselves. A cord of three strands is not quickly broken.
Ecclesiastes 4:12

Author's Reflections

When we peek into the future and struggle to see something to hope for or look forward to, it helps to have people around us to remind us of futures worth fighting for. In seasons of darkness, dismay, and despair, the enemy will try to convince us to go through life alone so we don't become a burden to others, but we need other people. We need other Christians to fight alongside us, to encourage us as we wait patiently for the Lord, to cry with us for deliverance.

The warrior bride is a corporate body, and if we are to be part of the Bride of Christ, we need to learn to both fellowship and fight with our brothers and sisters in Christ. Is there anything you're going through in this season that could use a bit of extra support in prayer from Christian friends and family? How can you be more intentional in reaching out to them for prayer?

The Loyal Ally

The dawn brought with it a brand new determination to get the scarlet woman out of the pit the guards had thrown her in. They weren't about to leave her behind, and this conviction circled the warrior princess's mind as she hopped off her bed before the sun could rise. They couldn't risk the scarlet woman being returned to her masters — not when the King of Light had already claimed her.

The warrior princess stepped out of her bedroom and found the inn empty. A soft smile appeared on her lips. This would give her time to quiet herself and try to hear from her King. She descended the wooden staircase and made her way outside the inn to observe a quiet alley in the heart of a city known for its darkness. She shuddered — partly because of the morning chill, partly because of the deep awareness that she was in a city where most did not submit themselves to the King's authority.

"Even here, I am present. Even here, I am sovereign."

It wasn't just the words but also Whom the voice had come from that soothed her soul like no other. There it was, His presence thick in its glory, surrounding her, within her, before her, behind her — hemming her in, reminding her of why she was there in the first place.

"I'm afraid," she admitted.

"WHY?"

"I don't know what to do. What if we fail her? She belongs to the light."

"WOULD I FAIL YOU?" She could hear the smile in His voice.

"Never."

"I WON'T START TODAY."

The warrior princess smiled. She had forgotten Who her confidence stemmed from. With one statement, He filled her heart yet again with the kind of confidence that could only come from Him.

"REMEMBER WHOSE CHILD SHE IS NOW THAT SHE HAS DECIDED TO FOLLOW THE LIGHT."

"Has she decided, though? She surrendered herself to the darkness without even consulting us first."

"ONLY BECAUSE SHE DOESN'T YET KNOW WHO SHE IS, WHO SHE CAN BE. REMIND HER. AS FOR WHETHER OR NOT SHE HAS DECIDED, SHE HAS BEEN FOLLOWING YOU, HASN'T SHE? YOU ARE LIGHT AS LONG AS YOU REMAIN IN ME."

The reminder both humbled and challenged her. "Forgive me for losing sight of You."

"YOU HAVEN'T. YOU MERELY SAW THE OBSTACLE STANDING BETWEEN YOU AND WHAT WAS PROMISED. TAKE HEART AND DO NOT WORRY ABOUT WHAT TO SAY TO THE GUARDS ONCE YOU REACH THE PIT. THE RIGHT WORDS WILL COME TO YOU AT THE RIGHT TIME."

"And what of our companions?"

"WHAT OF THEM?"

"Faith warned us of some who are not loyal to the kingdom."

"TAKE THEM TO MY KINGDOM. THE SORTING OUT WILL HAPPEN THERE IN DUE TIME."

The instruction eased the burden weighing heavy on her shoulders. "Thank you," she whispered to Him.

"Who are you talking to?"

The warrior princess drew a breath, almost as if to inhale His presence as a way of never letting go of Him, but He was still there with her. She believed because of His promise to never leave her nor forsake her. She turned her head to find their red-winged companion making his way to her.

She smiled at him. "Someone I would love for you to meet someday."

Manna

VERSES FOR MEDITATION

RUTH — GRIEVED: *But Ruth replied, "Don't urge me to leave you or to turn back from you. Where you go I will go, and where you stay I will stay. Your people will be my people and your God my God. Where you die I will die, and there I will be buried. May the Lord deal with me, be it ever so severely, if even death separates you and me."*
Ruth 1:16-17

*You hem me in behind and before,
and you lay your hand upon me.*
Psalm 139:5

*If I say, "Surely the darkness will hide me
and the light become night around me,"
even the darkness will not be dark to you;
the night will shine like the day,
for darkness is as light to you.*
Psalm 139:11-12

AUTHOR'S REFLECTIONS

He is the God Who stays. He is the God Who doesn't abandon us in our trouble, in our trials, in our battles. The King of Kings is the kind of King Who is mindful of His subjects. For those of us who have pledged fealty to Him, He is a loyal Friend, a faithful Ally.

We pray for people like Ruth who will be loyal to us and to the call and purpose God has for us, but throughout our lives, we discover that the loyalty of Ruth to Naomi is nowhere near comparable to the loyalty Christ has displayed at the cross. Jesus Himself — Ruler of the Universe — humbled Himself to be like us, to take upon Himself our likeness, to be tempted as we are tempted, to be with us even in the darkest of places, to take our place in the face of death. He was forsaken at the cross, yet we will never be as forsaken as He was, because He Himself promised to never leave us nor forsake us.

In seasons of loneliness and despair, remember Who your Loyal Ally is.

day 19

THE WINGS OF REDEMPTION

The red-winged warrior ignored what the warrior princess said and made his stance clear. "We should leave," he said. "She is not worth risking ourselves for. You heard what the guards said. She's a slave — one who is unclean."

The coldness in his tone and his words grieved the warrior princess's heart. "She sounds to me like the type of person who needs hope and redemption most. The good news proclaimed by the kingdom I belong to is anyone can have hope and be free."

"What's your plan then?"

"Do you know where they've taken her?"

"To the holding pits for the night. Her master has probably been informed of her capture. I wouldn't be surprised if someone has already been sent to claim her today."

"She is a child of light. She belongs to my King."

"That's not how it works."

"Take us to her, so we can dispute her capture. You might be surprised how powerful the King we serve truly is."

The red-winged warrior smirked. "I'll take you, but only because I want to see your face when you fail. The prince of darkness rules this city."

Yet we have brought His kingdom, an everlasting kingdom, here.

The warrior princess only smiled in response. She didn't need to defend her King. The winged one would see soon enough.

It didn't take long before the sentinel and the iron maiden awakened. The iron maiden opted to stay behind while the winged brothers carried the warrior princess and the sentinel to the holding pits — a dark, cavernous place where the rulers of darkness kept prisoners in deep, dank pits similar to the one the red-winged warrior had put the warrior princess and his brother in.

The guard at the entrance grimaced at the sight of them. "She belongs to her master," he said even before they could state why they had come.

"The King of light has ransomed and redeemed her," the warrior princess countered. "We have come to stake His claim on her."

The guard scoffed at her. "This is a city of darkness. It is not subject to light."

"The darkness may not comprehend light, but light will always continue to shine on darkness." The warrior princess smiled, her confidence growing with every word. "You do know what happens to night when day breaks through, right?"

The guard grimaced at her. "You are wasting my time with your empty platitudes. Go on your way. We will return her to her master by noon."

"No." The blind winged one stepped up. "By the laws of this city, you cannot execute judgment on her should someone take her under their wing. I take her under my wing until the city council makes a ruling on her behalf."

The warrior princess held her breath as the guard perused them with tired, apathetic eyes. He grunted. "Off to the council then."

"We must see her first," the warrior princess insisted. To her relief, the guard relented. At the edge of a deep, round pit, they called out to the scarlet woman. The prisoner lifted her face and took their breaths away, because where there used to be grief and desperation, joy and hope radiated.

Her countenance alone gave the warrior princess confidence that an astounding story of redemption was well on its way.

Manna

Verses for Meditation

RUTH — GRIEVED: *He said, "Who are you?" And she answered, "I am Ruth, your servant. Spread your wings over your servant, for you are a redeemer."*
Ruth 3:9 (ESV)

You are all children of the light and children of the day. We do not belong to the night or to the darkness.
1 Thessalonians 5:5

Jesus called them together and said, "You know that the rulers of the Gentiles lord it over them, and their high officials exercise authority over them. Not so with you...'
Matthew 20:25-26a

Author's Reflections

Scripture is filled with imagery of us being under the shelter of the Almighty's wings. When Ruth dared to approach Boaz to "spread his wings [cloak] over her" as a redeemer, it reflected the redeeming power of what Jesus did at the cross. By the ultimate sacrifice of Christ, we have been redeemed. Those who choose to follow Him are no longer under the rule of night and darkness, but under the rule of His kingdom.

This doesn't mean we do not submit to the earthly authorities over us — unless they require us to sin or disobey God — but it does mean we are under a higher law and covenant. The enemy will try to convince us we are still slaves to sin, slaves to our former nature, slaves to our flesh. We certainly have a choice to remain under the yoke of slavery, but we don't have to and we shouldn't! We have been granted freedom and power to overcome.

In times of contention — when all seems dark around us — let us always remember: Christ has redeemed us, and our redemption story will continue to play out as long as we live, if we continue to abide in Him.

day 20

REDEMPTION STORY

The scarlet woman emanated bright light as her smile widened at them. The warrior princess and the sentinel exchanged glances even as they reflected her brilliant smile. Even the blind brother — though he could not see — seemed to sense the surge of joy leaping from the pit of darkness toward them. Only the red-winged warrior bristled at the scene before them.

"Why do you smile?" he asked. "You are at the bottom of a pit, awaiting trial in the heart of darkness. You know what you are about to face, the things they would reveal about you to shame you, to justify keeping you in the darkness and away from the light."

"None of that matters anymore!" the scarlet woman exclaimed. "Messengers of light visited me in the night to minister to me. The citizens of light have been right all along! I have never been abandoned. His glory covers this place. That knowledge alone makes me believe I can hold my head up high, because no matter what happens — whether slave or free — I am among the redeemed."

With every word she spoke, the determination within the warrior princess grew. They had to do everything they could to get her out of there and accompany them along their journey into the light. "Grace and peace to you, woman of scarlet. It blesses our hearts to see your hope in our King. Today, we stand with you through this trial, believing in the King's ability to deliver you!"

"Thank you! I am grateful to find you didn't abandon me as well. How this trial goes, it matters not. Even when surrounded by darkness, the King's light is within me, and He has delivered me from death."

The delight in the heart of the warrior princess at the words of the scarlet woman turned into apprehension when she noticed the agitation on the sentinel's face. He lacked the confidence the woman had. Why?

<u>Why do you do this to yourself?</u>

The unwelcome voice made her flinch.

<u>You have no chance of freeing this woman. Why do you entertain her delusions?</u>

The warrior princess sighed. There was no way her adversary could shake her resolve to give the scarlet woman the best fight they could give to liberate her from the grips of darkness.

Encouraged by the scarlet woman's resilience and faith, the warrior princess ignored the red-winged warrior's doubts and the sentinel's worries. She headed to the city council with confidence the King's shield and glory had her covered. The scarlet woman would surely receive the freedom she had already been given.

Manna

VERSES FOR MEDITATION

RUTH — GRIEVED: *So Boaz took Ruth, and she became his wife. And he went in to her, and the Lord gave her conception, and she bore a son. Then the women said to Naomi, "Blessed be the Lord, who has not left you this day without a redeemer, and may his name be renowned in Israel! He shall be to you a restorer of life and a nourisher of your old age, for your daughter-in-law who loves you, who is more to you than seven sons, has given birth to him."*
Ruth 4:13-15 (ESV)

Many are saying of me,
"God will not deliver him."
But you, Lord, are a shield around me,
my glory, the One who lifts my head high.
Psalm 3:2-3

'Instead, whoever wants to become great among you must be your servant, and whoever wants to be first must be your slave— just as the Son of Man did not come to be served, but to serve, and to give his life as a ransom for many."
Matthew 20:26b-29

AUTHOR'S REFLECTIONS

Have you ever helped someone on their spiritual journey? Have you witnessed someone grow from the time of spiritual birth to the point of maturity, where they themselves came to a realization of their identity in Christ and can contend not only for their destiny but also for the destinies of others?

There is something beautiful and encouraging about seeing someone whom God has placed and entrusted under our wing develop from feeding on spiritual milk to digesting the meat of Scripture and living it out. It is such a privilege when God uses us that way!

Is there someone whom God has entrusted to you to care for until the point of spiritual maturity? How are you encouraging their growth and how have their stories of redemption encouraged you as a servant of God?

day 21

THE POOLS OF COMPROMISE

The court was in session. The city council — five of them — sat in seats at the front of the circular hall. In the middle was a round pedestal with metal railings around it and a short flight of steps leading up to it. It served as the stand for whomever was being given permission to address the council. To the right of the stand was a table where the men taking claim of the scarlet woman's life sat behind. To the left of the stand was where the warrior princess, the sentinel, and the blind winged one sat behind another table next to the scarlet woman. Behind them, a small crowd had gathered, among whom were the red-winged warrior, the iron maiden, and the rest of their group.

A man with a tired, grim face — seemingly suspicious of all who would dare enter his courtroom — sat at the center of the council. "Two parties are staking their claim over this woman," he said. "First, her masters, citizens of this city, who have had ownership of her since her youth. Second, these citizens of light claiming this slave as a child of another kingdom by virtue of a binding ransom treaty between the kingdom of light and the city of darkness. Who wishes to state their case first?"

The doors at the back of the room swung open and into the atrium-like hall strode a strikingly handsome being whose stately posture and extravagant clothing pegged him as a noteworthy figure.

At the sight of him, color drained from the council's faces. A collective gasp filled the room. The very sight of him made the blood of the warrior princess turn cold. He exuded a powerful darkness, causing everyone to leap to their feet to acknowledge his presence.

All but the children of light rose to their feet — a sign of respect for the stranger.

When his attention flitted from the warrior princess to the scarlet woman, fury and disgust crossed his face before a menacing smile lifted the corners of his mouth.

No one needed to tell her who this new arrival was. He was the prince of this city. The scarlet woman trembled next to the warrior princess, who immediately took hold of her hand.

"Don't be afraid," the warrior princess said — whether to herself or to the scarlet woman, she wasn't sure.

He confidently took the stand and waved for everyone to sit — not without his bottom lip curling at the kingdom children's refusal to stand in his presence. A hushed silence filled the room, accompanied by a distinct sense of fear present and increasing.

"I will speak," he said. His eyes roamed the entirety of the room before settling on the scarlet woman. Though handsome and alluring in appearance, there was no mistaking the spite he had for the defendant. "She is a slave of her masters, and a slave of this city. No one knows her history more than I, so I have personally come to make sure the darkness keeps what it rightfully owns." He leered at the scarlet woman. "The darkness had taken hold of this woman long before she became a slave, and I first made her acquaintance when I discovered her in quite a compromising position in the city's pools of pleasure."

As he continued to speak out his accusations against the scarlet woman, the warrior princess's determination faltered upon realizing how little she knew of all the compromises the daughter of enmity had made to draw her out of the light and into the darkness.

Manna

Verses for Meditation

Bathsheba — Shamed: *In the spring, at the time when kings go off to war, David sent Joab out with the king's men and the whole Israelite army. They destroyed the Ammonites and besieged Rabbah. But David remained in Jerusalem.*
2 Samuel 11:1

*Then I heard a loud voice in heaven say: "Now have come the salvation and the power
and the kingdom of our God,
and the authority of his Messiah.
For the accuser of our brothers and sisters,
who accuses them before our God day and night,
has been hurled down.*
Revelation 12:10

It is for freedom that Christ has set us free. Stand firm, then, and do not let yourselves be burdened again by a yoke of slavery.
Galatians 5:1

Author's Reflections

Some fights happen on the battlefield. Some happen in courts of legislation. The Bible tells us we have an accuser standing before God day and night, hurling accusations against us. This is why we need to be vigilant every day, because we have an enemy who refuses to stop his attacks on us and will use whatever means necessary to drag us down with him — whether by legal means or illegal.

Let us remember, however: our God is a just God. He is a Righteous Judge, full of mercy and compassion.

He knows us inside and out, so whatever the accusations the enemy hurls against us, we can still stand firm before our God — with all the freedom afforded us at the cross — and claim the righteousness and purity the blood of the Lamb grants us.

Is there anything the enemy is accusing you of right now? How can you stand firm in the freedom Christ has offered you?

day 22

A FATAL BEAUTY

Image upon image flashed within the minds of all who were present. The prince of darkness exposed lurid details of the scarlet woman's past — the men seduced, the troubles caused, the lives destroyed, the fortunes stolen — and what had brought her into slavery. Despite how convinced she was of the scarlet woman's right to enter the kingdom of light, the warrior princess couldn't suppress her shudders as the prince of darkness exposed all the reasons the scarlet woman belonged to the darkness.

"Who will pay the money she owes this city?" The prince of darkness squared his shoulders as he continued to leer at the woman accused. "Look at her. She is not even ashamed of all she has done. She lifts her head high and shows herself absent of remorse. Time and time again, her beauty has caused the most noble of our citizens to stumble, and she has continued to benefit from their downfall. When our good city sentenced her to slavery to account for all the wrong she has committed, she suddenly claims to be covered by the laws of light! This woman is one of the worst among us, and yet, these strangers demand her freedom! Why should we surrender to their kingdom what is rightfully ours?!"

An angry clamor for what they viewed as just punishment covered the courts. The citizens of darkness were out for blood — her blood. The warrior princess couldn't come up with a defense for her — not when she herself was aghast over all the things she had discovered about the woman she had been tasked to usher into the kingdom capital.

The prideful smirk on the prince of darkness's face as he finished stating his case filled the warrior princess with dread. What was she doing in a place like this, standing in defense of one of the worst of sinners?

"Who speaks on behalf of the slave?" the head of the council asked.

The warrior princess was about to rise, but the scarlet woman stood up instead. If she felt any shame at all at the accusations hurled against her, there was no evidence of it in her countenance. She still radiated the same light she had when they had found her in the pit earlier in the morning.

With a quiet dignity, she took the stand in place of the prince of darkness. Whispers of derision and disgusted utterances filled the room as she did, yet she stood her ground as she faced her accuser.

"It is true," she said. "I am among the worst of this city, and I have blood on my hands. This, I will not deny. I left the kingdom of light — the place of my birth and childhood — and spent my youth in this city, reckless and foolish. Throughout my time here, I have given in to dishonorable, despicable desires. It is true. Many have lost their lives because of my folly. These sojourners from my homeland gave me a vision of a new life and a brand new future. However, I cannot deny all that has been said against me. Of many of the accusations, I plead guilty."

Given the scarlet woman's statement and plea, the warrior princess's breath hitched as all hope of fulfilling their mission and getting this woman out of the city faded into the oblivion of the innumerable sins of the daughter of enmity.

Manna

Verses for Meditation

BATHSHEBA — SHAMED: *One evening David got up from his bed and walked around on the roof of the palace. From the roof he saw a woman bathing. The woman was very beautiful...*
2 Samuel 11:2

Beloved, I urge you as aliens and strangers [in this world] to abstain from the sensual urges [those dishonorable desires] that wage war against the soul.
1 Peter 2:11 (AMP)

Here is a trustworthy saying that deserves full acceptance: Christ Jesus came into the world to save sinners—of whom I am the worst.
1 Timothy 1:15

Author's Reflections

The truth is we are guilty. None of us are innocent according to the righteous standards of God. All of us fall short, and should we stand in a courtroom apart from God, we do not stand a chance against the accusations of the enemy. Why then do we continue to fight the good fight of faith?

Because through every temptation we have succumbed to, through every pitfall we have fallen into, through every sin we have committed, it doesn't change His character and His faithfulness. He is Christ. He is Messiah. Jesus came into the world to save us.

If we reflect on the history of the world and the barbaric society Christianity entered into, it is breathtaking to recognize what the cross saved us from. With the present state of the world — in all its corruption and compromise — and a future bleak in its progressive surrender to darkness, the hope Christ has given us for our eternal future is still an astounding reality, if we but take a moment to appreciate it.

May this be a reminder of how we are but sojourners passing through this world. No matter what comes our way in the coming decades, we still have the hope of glory — Christ in us!

THE LAMB WHO WAS SLAIN

The statements of the scarlet woman, the incredulous looks on the council's faces, the outrage of the audience, and the sneer on the prince's face might as well have sealed the guilty woman's fate. The warrior princess shook her head at the sentinel, whose fallen expression betrayed his sense of defeat. However, there was no way the warrior princess would accept a verdict other than freedom — not after the visitation she had with her King earlier that morning. He had made it clear to her the scarlet woman had chosen the light, and they were to take her to the kingdom of light. His Word had to stand no matter where they were, whether in places of darkness or of light.

The warrior princess stared at the scarlet woman with breathless anticipation. Surely she had more to say in her own defense other than she was guilty!

"Is there anything more you would like to say for yourself, scarlet woman?" the council head asked.

"The King of Light came to the dark pit where you imprisoned me. He has assured me of His forgiveness and mercy, even if I do not deserve it. It is only in Him that I take my stand and my plea for mercy. I put my trust in Him, so whatever consequences will result from this trial, it will be as He meant it to be, and I surrender to His ruling."

The disgusted sneers of the council did not give the warrior princess much hope this would turn out the way they wanted it to.

"Does anyone else wish to speak on both sides?" The council head scanned the faces of the crowd.

The warrior princess stood up on pure impulse. Something else had to be said on the scarlet woman's behalf. The moment she took the stand, she shut her eyes and asked for the right words to say.

"Speak." The council head prodded her with a dismissive wave of his hand. "What can you say on behalf of this woman?"

"There is a standing treaty between darkness and light. Whoever acknowledges the King's ransom and chooses to live in the ways of His kingdom will be absolved of all past sins, because all crimes have already been paid for via the atoning sacrifice of the innocent Lamb Who rules our Kingdom. The scarlet woman has chosen to be a child of the light."

The council head directed a questioning, contemptuous glare at the scarlet woman. "You acknowledge this ransom?"

The scarlet woman nodded, her eyes moist with tears. "I pledge my allegiance to the Lamb."

Murmurs filled the room, and it quickly turned into an outcry for justice. Surely one such as her could not escape the consequences of her folly! The once civil audience transformed into an angry mob, hurling insults and expletives her way.

To the surprise of the warrior princess, both winged brothers who were part of their party were quick to come to the scarlet woman's defense, covering her with their wings.

At the chaos sure to follow, the council head stood to his feet and demanded silence. When he did not receive it, he had to adjourn the hearing and set another date for the next day. The guards led the woman back to the pit, and the warrior princess and her group faced yet another night in the heart of this city of darkness.

Manna

Verses for Meditation

BATHSHEBA — SHAMED: *When Uriah's wife heard that her husband was dead, she mourned for him. After the time of mourning was over, David had her brought to his house, and she became his wife and bore him a son. But the thing David had done displeased the Lord.*
2 Samuel 11:26-27

*He lifted me out of the slimy pit,
out of the mud and mire;
he set my feet on a rock
and gave me a firm place to stand.
He put a new song in my mouth,
a hymn of praise to our God.
Many will see and fear the Lord
and put their trust in him.*
Psalm 40:2-3

But when they arrest you, do not worry about what to say or how to say it. At that time you will be given what to say, for it will not be you speaking, but the Spirit of your Father speaking through you.
Matthew 10:19-20

Author's Reflections

People often complain about the unfairness of life, without realizing that if life was fair, we would have to answer for all our transgressions and trespasses. There is a heart-breaking and frustrating darkness in the unfairness of life, that much is certain, but there is also beauty in what seems unfair in our eyes. Unfair means God will not make us pay for the full measure of our sins. It means we can have a greater reward and enjoy a life we don't deserve.

Have you ever done anything which might have deserved punishment, but God cleared your name and delivered you from the consequences of your folly? Can you think of anyone in your life who may deserve a certain negative outcome because of their choices in life, but you've seen God's mercy continue to rescue them from sure destruction? How can you extend mercy to yourself and to others the same way the Righteous Judge does?

A Sensitive Predicament

Silence filled the inn as they all lost themselves in their thoughts, huddled together in a cozy sitting area beside a crackling furnace. None of the three leaders, the kingdom children, and the two brothers wished to leave that spot and retreat to their rooms for some rest. After having escaped the courtroom and the rage of the people demanding the scarlet woman's blood, every single one of them longed for the comfort of company they could trust, company who would wish them no harm.

"They hate us," one of the children eventually croaked out.

"He's right." Another child spoke up with a quivering voice. "How can we be safe in a city such as this? Why must we fight for the woman in red? Let us go on our way and see ourselves out of here before their hatred of her becomes their hatred of us."

One by one, all seven of the children agreed it would be best if they all went ahead without the scarlet woman.

The iron maiden sighed. "I hate to agree, but we've already lost a blind man on the way to this city. We can afford to lose another if it means we complete our mission by bringing all the others to the capital."

"No." The sentinel shook his head. "We cannot abandon her. It will be the death of her."

"It will be the death of us if we stay!" The red-winged warrior said the words through gritted teeth.

"I'd like to stay and see this through," the blind winged one said. "I know what it is like to be trapped in a pit without hope. To deal with the pain of abandonment is not something I would wish on anyone."

"She has brought this upon herself," the seeing brother responded. "Why should we all suffer for the reckless life she lived?"

"You are no less deserving than her! You have committed crimes as well. Why should she be punished and you get to go free? How can you receive mercy and not be willing to give it to those who ask for it?" With those words, the blind silenced the seeing.

"Some can go, and some should stay," the iron maiden suggested. "There are three of us tasked to fulfill this mission. The winged warrior and I can lead the children past the city walls to the capital while you, the sentinel, and the blind winged one stay to wait for the outcome of the trial."

"That's a fair compromise," the sentinel said. "It seems the wise thing to do, but Faith did say we can't get past the gates unless we're complete."

"She didn't know about the scarlet woman when she gave us the warning." Desperation oozed out of the iron maiden's lips. "Maybe there will be an exception."

"Even so, we cannot split up; otherwise, you'll only be left waiting for us at the gates," the warrior princess said.

Something stirred the spirit of the warrior princess, telling her they were better off together than apart. As long as they could gather and draw strength from one another, they had a better chance of reaching the capital. However, the distress among them was palpable, so the warrior princess offered a compromise. "Let's stay another night and wait until morning to decide," she said, hoping they would agree. To her relief, they did. That gave her time to spend the hours of the night seeking instruction from her Lord and Ruler so she could welcome the morning knowing what they should do.

Manna

Verses for Meditation

BATHSHEBA — SHAMED: *Then David said to Nathan, "I have sinned against the Lord."*

Nathan replied, "The Lord has taken away your sin. You are not going to die. But because by doing this you have shown utter contempt for the Lord, the son born to you will die."
2 Samuel 12:13–14

If the world hates you, keep in mind that it hated me first. If you belonged to the world, it would love you as its own. As it is, you do not belong to the world, but I have chosen you out of the world. That is why the world hates you.
John 15:18–19

So speak encouraging words to one another. Build up hope so you'll all be together in this, no one left out, no one left behind. I know you're already doing this; just keep on doing it.
1 Thessalonians 5:11 (MSG)

Author's Reflections

Hatred toward Christians has grown over the last decades, and it will continue to grow as the return of the Lord draws near. Our message isn't a politically correct one nowadays, and the threat of worldwide persecution looms over our heads as the eleventh hour of the Lord's return draws near. This shouldn't surprise us. Christ warned His disciples of this, and every generation has experienced this reality over the past two thousand years.

How do we respond?

There is something beautiful that happens to the church amid persecution. We come together, and as long as we can, we should not give up in gathering together and encouraging one another. There's something about the gathering of the saints that gives us hope despite what's to come, and we all have a better chance of enduring to the end if we don't give up on encouraging one another to continue to fight the good fight of faith for and with one another.

day 25

THE POWER SOURCE

The candle flickered as the wick burned through the wax, the source of light dwindling as the warrior princess burned the night hours in pursuit of wisdom and direction concerning the journey ahead. Should they break apart? Was this their only recourse? Was this the way they should go? Though it made sense, why did she feel so ill at ease regarding the matter? Would they understand if she pulled rank as leader of the group and demanded they all stay together and accompany the scarlet woman as she awaited her verdict?

The silence of the night mocked her. His voice was nowhere to be heard, His presence nowhere to be seen. What was she to do? As the night wore on, the darkness magnified the sense of powerlessness growing within her. The exhaustion was taking over and the longing for sleep and rest was making her eyes droop, but she fought hard to stay awake. She needed to intercede on behalf of the scarlet woman, to seek her Lord's heart regarding the situation. Her spirit longed for this! Surely she could go another hour!

In an attempt to stay alert and keep her wits about her, she rose to her feet and paced the floor, keenly aware of how weak her body was compared to the strength of desire and power of will coursing through her spirit.

She sighed. Many times before, she had overcome by His Spirit, not her own. Surely, she could overcome again

— especially considering the urgency of the situation at hand.

"What are you doing?" The small, but familiar, voice jolted her senses awake.

The warrior princess turned toward the direction of the voice. Her mouth dropped open at the little winged figure fluttering in the air in front of her. "Folly?" She blinked her eyes several times to make sure she hadn't just given in to some sort of delusion that this friend whom she had once traveled with in the wilderness was really present.

"It is me!" Folly twirled in the air, her gossamer wings glittering and fluttering behind her. "It has been a long time, hasn't it?"

"It has! How are you doing? How did you find me? What has been happening among the creatures of the wilderness since I entered the kingdom?"

Folly threw her arms in the air. "So many questions! I will answer them in due time, but not right now. First, I no longer go by the name Folly, but Faith."

The news was a sure source of delight to the warrior princess. As a woman in the wilderness, she had once prayed for this! "I am pleased to hear that, and it is a pleasure to see a friend from the wilderness in a place like this."

Faith scanned their surroundings and nodded. "We can agree on that! But, before we get further distracted, just like you, I must stay on mission and not get sidetracked. I have been sent to remind you of the source of your power, warrior princess."

"The source of my power? Have I forgotten?"

Faith smiled. "You asked for wisdom for the journey ahead, and the King has sent me here to deliver."

Manna

VERSES FOR MEDITATION

BATHSHEBA — SHAMED: *Then David comforted his wife Bathsheba, and he went to her and made love to her. She gave birth to a son, and they named him Solomon. The Lord loved him*
2 Samuel 12:24

Then he returned to his disciples and found them sleeping. "Simon," he said to Peter, "are you asleep? Couldn't you keep watch for one hour? Watch and pray so that you will not fall into temptation. The spirit is willing, but the flesh is weak."
Mark 14:37-38

Whoever trusts in his own mind is a fool, but he who walks in wisdom will be delivered.
Proverbs 28:26 (ESV)

AUTHOR'S REFLECTIONS

The world needs more watchmen and intercessors, those who are willing to set aside time to contend and shed tears for the many concerns plaguing the world. There is no preparing to be the Bride of Christ without immersing ourselves in this discipline. After all, this is one of the most effective ways by which we fight our battles. On our knees.

We learn to accompany our Lord and Savior, Who Himself interceded for us, standing as the High Priest in the order of Melchizedek to make a way for us to approach the throne of grace.

Let us stay vigilant in these days to draw near to the Lord and intercede for our loved ones, our homes, our cities, our nations. Let us be expectant for His answers!

It may not look like we imagine. Sometimes, God answers us through the most unexpected of sources. He delivers what we ask for using unlikely people or situations. No matter how He answers, rest assured He is listening, and He will answer!

The Unlovely Bride

Faith's shoulders heaved up and down as she took several deep breaths, her wings fluttering as she glided in the air, back and forth, to and fro. Her every motion reminded the warrior princess of her time spent in the wilderness with the little pixie-like creature; however, this time, there was no denying the transformation from Folly to Faith. Gone were the belligerent harrumphs and unreserved grimaces of a Folly rebellious against the King and His creatures. Faith's current mannerisms had a certain grace about it. She had a calm confidence that had been absent then, present now.

The sight of her brought tears to the warrior princess's eyes. Surely the King was faithful to change anyone who would ask Him to!

Finally, Faith stopped her pacing through the air and fixed herself in one spot, right in front of the warrior princess. She rolled her eyes as if in an attempt to recall something. She lifted her forefinger in the air as she recited the message she was supposed to deliver to the warrior princess. "The King has been pleased by your faithfulness throughout your journey in seeking His face and asking for His wisdom and strength. He wishes to remind you this is where your power lies — in your constant resolve to seek Him. You are exactly where He wants you to be. Be encouraged. He has heard your pleas and will intervene in due time. Rest assured, He will not delay. Everything will happen according to His timeline — no later, no sooner."

The warrior princess smiled as the words Faith delivered proved to be the assurance she needed to face tomorrow. "Thank you for delivering the message, Faith. Is that all you came to say? Because I can't wait to hear about you and everything you've gone through since we last saw each other."

Faith huffed — an endearing picture of how remnants of her old personality still lingered in this new version of her. She crossed her arms against her chest. "Haven't you been listening? Everything in due time! Right now, I have a story to tell you."

"A story?"

"If you can find in you enough wakefulness to listen." Faith gestured toward the seat beside the burning furnace, facing the dying light of the candle.

"I'm too curious to fall asleep. You can be quite entertaining when you wish to be."

Faith grinned. "I'll take that as a compliment." She settled herself on top of the table, with the candle — about half her height — casting a glow on her face. "Okay. What was the story again?" She wrinkled her nose. "Oh yeah! It is the story of the unlovely bride. You must listen very well."

The warrior princess cast her old friend a soft smile. "I'm listening."

"And so, we begin..."

Manna

Verses for Meditation

Leah — Unwanted: *Now Laban had two daughters; the name of the older was Leah, and the name of the younger was Rachel. Leah had weak eyes, but Rachel had a lovely figure and was beautiful. Jacob was in love with Rachel*
Genesis 29:16-18a

Now God has us where he wants us, with all the time in this world and the next to shower grace and kindness upon us in Christ Jesus.
Ephesians 2:7 (MSG)

Look to the Lord and his strength; seek his face always.
1 Chronicles 16:11

Author's Reflections

The world around us always seems to be in a rush. Hustle culture tells us to make the most of every minute in terms of reaching our goals, becoming productive, and establishing our success. Everything is fast-paced. We are told that if we blink, there's a great chance we will miss out on something.

As people of kingdom culture, the rush and the hustle aren't things we promote or encourage. We are, of course, to be faithful stewards of our time, making sure the works of our hands are worthy offerings to a God Who loves to look at His creation and find it is good. However, whenever we are rushing and pressure mounts to get things done fast so we could get to the next thing, the next place, the next level of success, often times, this is a sign we need to take pause. Selah. Why the rush? God has His timeline. It will do us well to move according to His timing.

When we stay rooted in kingdom culture and in abiding relationship with the King, there is no need for this pressure, this hustle, this rush. We can rest in Him, and when we do, we discover that's where our strength lies. If His Word is true, it's the best way for us to live lives of fruitfulness — abiding in the Vine.

THE SCORNED WIFE

The story of Faith unfolded as she relayed it to the warrior princess with animated gestures and varying tones in her voice to emphasize her points and her lines of dialog. The warrior princess found it to be quite an enjoyable performance as she immersed herself in the story of this unlovely bride.

"She wasn't the one he wanted, but they had been betrothed through the machinations of her father. Neither of them could back out from the promised union even if he had eyes for another, and she was aware of it. It didn't take long for her to realize how much he hated her, because when he looked at her, he only viewed her as the hindrance between him and the bride he wanted.

"The unlovely bride served her husband as best she could. After all, this was what the kingdom taught her. She tried to be a good wife to him, but the more she tried, the more he despised her. When she gave birth to their son, she hoped it would somehow forge a bond between her and her husband, but though he loved and doted on their child, he still treated her with willful contempt. Eventually, he left the kingdom and started chasing after other lovers. Still, she tried to remain faithful and pour out her love and devotion toward the husband who didn't want her and the child they both adored.

"Because her husband viewed her as unlovely, she did everything possible to become a beauty in his eyes.

No matter what she did, he still couldn't stand the sight of her; other men, however, began to take notice. One in particular — a powerful figure in this city — took notice of her while she was bathing in a pool. He seduced her away from the kingdom of light and brought her to his bed. Obsessed with her beauty, he gave orders to have her husband and child killed."

A flicker of familiarity sparked in the mind of the warrior princess. Hadn't the prince of darkness mentioned finding the scarlet woman in pools of pleasure?

A sad smile appeared on Faith's face as she nodded to confirm the warrior princess's suspicions. The unlovely bride was the scarlet woman.

"We often see God's creations as they are in front of us, basing our impressions on their outward appearances and what they choose to reveal to us," Faith said. "But we must see beyond that, because there is always a story behind every person, and we cannot exact judgment on them without seeing the complete picture. This is why only the King can stand as a Righteous Judge, for only He sees all situations, as well as a person's heart, through and through."

The warrior princess brushed a tear away from her face as her heart ached on the scarlet woman's behalf.

"Shall I continue?" Faith asked.

The warrior princess nodded, and so she discovered the story behind why the scarlet woman had been given over to darkness.

Manna

VERSES FOR MEDITATION

LEAH — UNWANTED: *When the Lord saw that Leah was not loved, he enabled her to conceive, but Rachel remained childless.*
Genesis 29:31

Therefore God gave them over in the sinful desires of their hearts to sexual impurity for the degrading of their bodies with one another.
Romans 1:24

Has not the one God made you? You belong to him in body and spirit. And what does the one God seek? Godly offspring. So be on your guard, and do not be unfaithful to the wife of your youth.
Malachi 2:15

But the Lord said to Samuel, "Do not consider his appearance or his height, for I have rejected him. The Lord does not look at the things people look at. People look at the outward appearance, but the Lord looks at the heart."
1 Samuel 16:7

AUTHOR'S REFLECTIONS

We are guilty. None of us are innocent. This is true. We all fall short. However, God also sees the wounds inflicted on us by a battle-weary world and a relentless adversary. He sees past what others see and knows our very depths. He is not blind to the scars we have endured and the open wounds still gaping within us — unhealed because of constant re-opening through ongoing pain.

We do not encourage a victim mentality in the kingdom of God, but we also must acknowledge the roots of our vagrant desires and our straying thoughts. This is not so we can justify our sins with the reasoning that we have once been hurt and oppressed, but so we can uproot the weeds of destruction the enemy has placed in our lives to keep us from reaching full maturity in Christ.

This is a process a lot of us avoid — Christian or not. We try to escape dealing with the wounds of the past and releasing forgiveness where it is due. To progress in our spiritual walk, however, we cannot allow any foothold of bitterness, resentment, or trauma to remain in our lives. Not when God has promised to set us free from all of these!

Let us, however, remain gracious toward ourselves, because God is gracious to us. As we go through this process, let us remember He sees us. He knows us. He is at work in us, and it is up to Him to finish what He has started in us.

day 28

SOUL GAMES

As Faith continued to tell the story of the scarlet woman, the warrior princess got a fuller picture of the truth behind the woman they were fighting for.

"Heart-broken, she swore to herself she would never experience such pain again, so when the prince of darkness offered her protection and power for her loyalty — that she would always do his bidding — she agreed. She did all sorts of evil under his control. In exchange, he protected her from the consequences of her crimes. He gave her influence and wealth, and she continued to play his games and do his bidding. All the while, she planned her revenge against him. After all, he was the very person who had stolen her husband and child from her. It took years before she saw an opportunity to stab him in the back.

"He was still, however, much more powerful than she had anticipated. After her betrayal, he set out to destroy her life, to expose her for all the things she had done for him, but washing his hands of all of it in the process. She took the fall for all his dark devises and machinations." The expression on Faith's face darkened as she relayed all the violence the scarlet woman suffered at the hands of the prince of darkness. "She paid for all the crimes she had committed on his behalf by being sentenced to slavery, under men controlled by the prince himself.

He prostituted her and subjected her to all types of humiliation. Her soul was his to toy with.

"She had been at the mercy of his indulgences and whims for years, and the prince of this city is not known to have a merciful bone in him. She has suffered much, and it was at a moment of utter despair that you came upon her."

The warrior princess's breath hitched as she recalled the expression on the scarlet woman's face when they had passed by her. Had all of it been by chance or by the plans and purposes of a King Who knew when and where to find and recover His flock?

"Only seconds before you came for her," Faith continued her story, "she cried out to the wind in hopes that it would carry her cries to the King of light. She swore fealty to Him — her life His to do with — if He would but rescue her from darkness."

"Is that why the King allowed us to go through this city instead of giving us safe passage straight to His capital? Was it for her sake?"

Faith smiled and gave the warrior princess a shrug. "That's for Him to know, but isn't it nice to think He is careful and concerned with the lives of all His subjects, even the ones who stray?"

The warrior princess reflected Faith's sweet smile even as an enduring love swept over her for all the children of the kingdom the King had entrusted her with, and as she reflected on His love, a song of praise flowed out of her lips.

Manna

Verses for Meditation

Leah — Unwanted: *Leah became pregnant and gave birth to a son. She named him Reuben, for she said, "It is because the Lord has seen my misery. Surely my husband will love me now."*
Genesis 29:32

Remember the former things, those of long ago;
I am God, and there is no other;
I am God, and there is none like me.
I make known the end from the beginning,
from ancient times, what is still to come.
I say, 'My purpose will stand,
and I will do all that I please.'
From the east I summon a bird of prey;
from a far-off land, a man to fulfill my purpose.
What I have said, that I will bring about;
what I have planned, that I will do.
Isaiah 46:9-11

for it is God who works in you to will and to act in order to fulfill his good purpose.
Philippians 2:13

Author's Reflections

Most of us have experienced the pain of rejection and the sorrow of neglect and abandonment. Most know what it is like to feel like we don't belong, like we're outcasts. We ask why we have to go through these things. Whether we deserve it or not, why does God — a loving Father — allow His children to be wounded by the world, and sometimes, even by His other children?

More often than not, we don't see the big picture. We don't see things like He does. We view life — ours and others' — through tunnel vision. God allows certain things for a reason, for a purpose, and we may not understand — we may even rage at Him for those times we have been neglected and abandoned — but His purposes stand. Because we are His people, His children, His subjects, we can trust His intentions for us are good.

Is there an area in your life where you are lacking in, where you wish He would come through for you, but hasn't? Are you able to still give Him your heart and trust Him with or without what you are asking for? Can you trust that even this heartache He can use for good?

day 29

A Heart of Praise

The animated expressions of Faith remained on her face as she calmed down and sat akimbo on top of the table, her palms cupping her cheeks as she listened to the warrior princess sing. It was this scene of reverent submission and unabashed adoration toward the King that her companions, one-by-one, woke up to. First, the sentinel, then the iron maiden, then the winged brothers, then each of the kingdom children. All gathered around her and joined her in praise.

Faith blew out the candle's waning flame as the first rays of the morning sun streamed through the window. A satisfied sigh escaped her lips.

Meanwhile, the warrior princess released all the pent-up pressure within her and offered it up to a King Who cared. All the voices that joined her as she sang were a sweet addition to the sincere echoes of her heart choosing to praise the King of Light in a place of darkness.

By the time they sang out their last note in unison, the heart of the warrior princess had already awakened with a burning love for not only the people surrounding her, but the scarlet woman. This wasn't just about fulfilling a mission anymore. Her heart ached for this person yearning for hope and salvation.

"This is how the King found her when He visited her at the pit of destruction to assure her of her status as a subject of His kingdom," Faith explained. "She was singing praise, a few kingdom songs she learned before she left the light for darkness. He cares for her, the same way He cares for each of us here." A wistful smile lightened Faith's countenance, her gaze lowered as if she was lost in a pleasant memory from another time.

It begged the curiosity of the warrior princess. She tilted her head to the side. "This is my friend, Faith," she introduced the little winged one to the others. "I know her from my time in the wilderness when she was still known as Folly. She still hasn't told me how she had transformed from Folly to Faith."

"I would love to tell you the story, but more urgent matters are at hand. Suffice it to say, the King never gave up on me. He kept sending His people to search me out and help me, to deliver me from my reckless ways. The gossamer prince and his bride, the troubadour, the sycamore, Lady Wisdom—" Faith nodded her head at the warrior princess "—you. Many have been a part of the change you see in me."

The iron maiden took a deep breath. "I guess that means we shouldn't give up on the scarlet woman either. We should stay to help her."

To the warrior princess's relief and surprise, one by one, everyone agreed. The only thing each one needed to overcome the fear and worry over their situation was a heart of praise.

Manna

Verses for Meditation

Leah — Unwanted: *She conceived again, and when she gave birth to a son she said, "This time I will praise the Lord." So she named him Judah. Then she stopped having children.*
Genesis 29:35

Let us not become weary in doing good, for at the proper time we will reap a harvest if we do not give up.
Galatians 6:9

Look at the birds of the air; they do not sow or reap or store away in barns, and yet your heavenly Father feeds them. Are you not much more valuable than they?
Matthew 6:26

I appeal to you, brothers and sisters, in the name of our Lord Jesus Christ, that all of you agree with one another in what you say and that there be no divisions among you, but that you be perfectly united in mind and thought.
1 Corinthians 1:10

Author's Reflections

A powerful shift happens within us when we lift our praises to God no matter what our circumstances are — even through disappointment. This is what Leah experienced in the book of Genesis. Her husband, Jacob, still loved her sister over her — even if she had already given him three sons, and Rachel had given him none. When Leah gave birth to Judah, something shifted in her and this is evident in the name she had given him:

Judah — "this time I will praise the Lord". Her situation was the same, but her heart changed. Her concerns and focus changed, as she directed them towards God.

We are in a better position to come together as Christians if we find ways to praise the Lord in unity, to worship Him, to glorify Him, to focus on Him and not on our own opinions, mindsets, and thinking. A heart of praise will seek His face and desire His thoughts, His heart, His ways. A heart of praise will surrender to Him in moments of uncertainty and perhaps even fear.

Do you have a heart of praise?

day 30

An Honored Life

United in spirit and purpose, the kingdom representatives returned to the council's court with a firm resolve to do everything in their power to get the scarlet woman out of the darkness and into the light. However, even if the sun had just risen, they reached the council's court to find the scarlet woman blindfolded and being dragged out into a public clearing where an angry crowd had already gathered.

The warrior princess rushed forward, the sentinel close behind her. "What is going on here?!" she demanded.

"The verdict has been given in your absence," a guard trying to control the rowdy crowd said. "She is to be put to death for the crimes she has committed as a citizen of this city. The execution will happen immediately."

"No! She is a child of our kingdom; this city has no authority to take her life."

The guard's lips curled at her words. "Take it up with the council. You shouldn't have been late. Perhaps you could have said something to defend her if you had shown up on time."

"We were not informed of the change in schedule. Why had the proceedings gone earlier than arranged?"

The guard shrugged. "It was moved up at the request of the prince."

Someone cleared his throat behind the warrior princess and before she could even turn to find out who it was, she already knew because a dark presence, all too familiar to her, filled her with dread. The dark prince was standing right beside her, his shoulder brushing against hers.

"She will die right before your eyes, princess," he said. "Her life will end in dishonor and shame."

"Why do you seem delighted by this injustice?"

"It is not an injustice. My accusations are all true, and she has admitted this. Only you refuse to give up on her and leave this city. She is not worthy of your concern."

"She is a subject of the King."

The prince's sneer made her shudder. "Then He should come here and save her, should he not? If she's so important, why does He stay in His city of light and not rescue her Himself?"

The warrior princess did not have a ready answer, but in her mind, a fearsome possibility roiled. A shiver climbed her body. Was this what she was supposed to do? Was this why the King had sent her? She searched her heart for a sliver of fear over what she was about to do. She found none other than the fear of failing to do what her King had tasked her to do.

"He doesn't have to come here, because He has already sent me," the warrior princess said. "The woman of scarlet will one day be dressed in white, shining with glorious light." Time and time again, she had seen the accused woman humble herself in surrender to the Lord. The King's edicts remained true. "She will live a long and prosperous life."

The prince laughed. "Is that so? And who, pray tell, will pay for her crimes? You?"

There was not a hint of hesitation in the warrior princess's tone. "Yes. I will willingly lay my life down for hers if you assure me that in doing so, all who are in my company — the kingdom citizens, the winged brothers, the scarlet woman, and all who wish to join them will be given safe passage out of this city, so they can reach the kingdom capital."

"The righteous warrior princess of the King in exchange for a common whore." The prince's smile grew wide. "You have yourself a deal."

Manna

Verses for Meditation

LEAH — UNWANTED: *There Abraham and his wife Sarah were buried, there Isaac and his wife Rebekah were buried, and there I buried Leah.*
Genesis 49:31

Humility is the fear of the LORD; its wages are riches and honor and life.
Proverbs 22:4

The grass withers, the flower fades, but the word of our God will stand forever.
Isaiah 40:8

Greater love has no one than this: to lay down one's life for one's friends.
John 15:13

Author's Reflections

The curse of sin and death has been plaguing the world for ages. We have witnessed death surround us — many falling by our side — and it is ever increasing, even as the days grow darker. War, famine, disease, plagues, natural disasters... on and on it goes — a constant reminder that life is fragile and fleeting.

When faced with death, do we tremble or do we remember this life we live is not our own, anyway? We have already surrendered it to our King. This is why we do not fear. We can follow Him to the ends of the earth. We can obey Him even unto death, because we've already died to our self and our flesh, anyway.

God is raising up a company of warriors in His church who will rise up unafraid of death. They will advance His kingdom to the far reaches of the world, and they will do this not through sword, shield, or strength, but by the power of the Spirit and the promise of His enduring Word.

Are you willing to be one of those whom He'll raise up in these last days to bring the Good News to the many who are yet to hear it? Would you be willing to obey, even if it costs you your life?

A Disguised Blessing

The dark prince's pronouncement that the warrior princess had volunteered to give her life for the scarlet woman's shocked both the citizens of darkness and the citizens of light. No one could believe she would do such a thing, least of all the scarlet woman.

When they were given a moment to speak in private in a small room the guards had shoved them into, the scarlet woman begged her not to push through with this. "You don't have to! I am resigned to my fate," she said. "It is enough for me that the King has brought me back into the light. Surely, your life is more precious than mine."

The warrior princess shook her head. "No one's life is more precious than another's. The King Himself laid down His life as a ransom for all who choose to be His subject, yet He lives. He will rescue us from death." She cupped her friend's face with her palms. "I am the one He sent for your rescue. He has sent me here to die in your place, so you could have eternal life. It may not make sense, but I understand now. This is my fight. This is why I have come here. I'm doing all of this for love."

Tears rushed down the scarlet woman's cheek. "If no life is more precious than anyone else's, then why should you give your life for mine? Why shouldn't I just face the consequences of my folly?"

"Because trust me when I say this is a blessing in disguise." The warrior princess smiled. "The dark prince is after me, not you."

A loud knock on the bolted door interrupted their conversation.

"It's time!" one guard yelled. Keys jangled outside the door and the click of the lock told them their time together would soon be over.

The warrior princess wiped the tears of the scarlet woman away. "It will be okay."

The door swung open, and the guards grabbed hold of the warrior princess.

"This can't happen!" The sentinel rushed toward her. The guards shoved him away.

"He's right," the iron maiden said. "There must be some other way."

"We will see each other again," the warrior princess promised, trying to reassure them.

"Faith said we couldn't get past the gates unless we're complete," the iron maiden objected.

"You are complete. The dark prince has assured us safe passage. It will not do him well to go back on his word. The moment they end my life, flee. Leave this city and take refuge in the King's light."

That was when the warrior princess saw it. A flicker of understanding — not in the faces of her fellow leaders, but in the eyes of the red-winged warrior. His confusion disappeared, and he nodded toward her.

"Make sure they get to the kingdom," she told him.

"I will." He gave her a nod.

They led her to a platform. A hush filled the square. None of them were angry now. Most were confused. In front of the crowd, standing close to the platform, the prince of darkness gave her an arrogant smirk. "Finally. I have defeated you."

"You have not taken anything that hasn't been given freely."

Confusion masked his handsome features and brought about his true image — a fiery dragon out to destroy everything in his path.

"I've already won over you twice, dragon," the warrior princess said. "Don't think this is any different."

"I am about to take the life of His Betrothed." His face darkened, his visage angry. "This is my victory."

The warrior princess smiled at him before scanning the faces of the crowd standing witness to her death. If only they all knew how loved they were! The executioner lifted the sword and pointed it at her. As it sliced through her, she welcomed the darkness only because still within her was the breaking through of a great light. The faint yell of a defeated adversary was the last thing she could remember before all consciousness escaped her.

When she opened her eyes, she awakened marked as the King's warrior bride.

Manna

VERSES FOR MEDITATION

MARY — RISKED: *In the sixth month of Elizabeth's pregnancy, God sent the angel Gabriel to Nazareth, a town in Galilee, to a virgin pledged to be married to a man named Joseph, a descendant of David. The virgin's name was Mary. The angel went to her and said, "Greetings, you who are highly favored! The Lord is with you."*
Luke 1:26-28

This is how we know what love is: Jesus Christ laid down his life for us. And we ought to lay down our lives for our brothers and sisters.
1 John 3:16

For if we have been united with him in a death like his, we will certainly also be united with him in a resurrection like his.
Romans 6:5

AUTHOR'S REFLECTIONS

For us to be a pure bride, ready for the return of our King, there must be in us a willingness to die, if that is what is required.

This may be figurative. We should die to self and kill the flesh, so to speak. We exhibit our love by laying down our lives here on earth in service to others, putting others first, with us being less and Him more.

This may also be literal. Many will be called as martyrs, ready to physically die, trusting their belief in Christ has granted them eternal life, and this is what awaits them on the other side of eternity.

Either way, if this is what the King asks of us, we do not tremble in fear, nor do we groan about our weakness. Death, after all, has lost its sting, for we are anchored by an everlasting and enduring hope.

So, we can face death with a smile and a firm conviction that we are about to step into the light of His glory.

day 32

A Servant Heart

She was no longer in the city of darkness. This much she knew to be true. The way her spirit lifted the moment she regained consciousness told her she was somewhere else, entirely — somewhere she had never been, but it still felt like home.

The warrior bride got up from a large bed. She, from the inside-out, had a strong sense of being light and free. She scanned her surroundings and found herself in a lavish room with ornate pearl walls and a high, arched ceiling. From the tall windows, a stream of generous light flooded the spacious bedroom.

Where was she? How had she gotten here?

The fine silk of the nightdress she wore brushed against her skin. She lifted the hem of her shift to look at the intricate embroidery and lace hanging from the silk. She had never worn such fine clothing in her entire life. Wherever she was, she was in a place of abundance. For reasons beyond her understanding, this unsettled her.

Tall mahogany doors swung open, and the warrior bride shrieked with delight at the sight of the scarlet woman. She skipped forward and pulled her friend into an embrace. They both shed tears as they hugged each other tightly.

"Thank you," the scarlet woman whispered. "It would be my honor to serve you and serve alongside you for the rest of my life. Because of your sacrifice, I have been given a brand-new life."

The scarlet woman's words brought about the recollection of what she had done. This was the person she had given her life for. The remembrance of the final lingering image in her head shook her. She had died. She had felt the sword slice through her, the breath leaving her. Why then was she breathing?

An object that appeared misplaced inside her room caught her attention. Right by the bed she had just risen from was a sword. Was it the very one the executioner had used to end her life?

"You'll get answers soon enough, for Faith and the iron maiden are on their way here to tell you of all the King has done on your behalf." The scarlet woman held both her hands to assure her. "I, on the other hand, have been sent as your handmaiden, to serve you, and provide for you whatever you need that you may be prepared for the coming of the King."

Beyond the seed of apprehension within her, the warrior bride's heart swelled at the information the scarlet woman had given her. "Does this mean—"

The scarlet woman smiled. "Yes. You are in the capital, my dear friend. You are finally in the palace of the King."

Manna

VERSES FOR MEDITATION

MARY — RISKED: *"I am the Lord's servant," Mary answered. "May your word to me be fulfilled." Then the angel left her.*
Luke 1:38

When the perishable has been clothed with the imperishable, and the mortal with immortality, then the saying that is written will come true: "Death has been swallowed up in victory."

*"Where, O death, is your victory?
Where, O death, is your sting?"*

The sting of death is sin, and the power of sin is the law. But thanks be to God! He gives us the victory through our Lord Jesus Christ.
1 Corinthians 15:57

And why do you worry about clothes? See how the flowers of the field grow. They do not labor or spin. Yet I tell you that not even Solomon in all his splendor was dressed like one of these. If that is how God clothes the grass of the field, which is here today and tomorrow is thrown into the fire, will he not much more clothe you—you of little faith?
Matthew 6:28-30

Each of you should use whatever gift you have received to serve others, as faithful stewards of God's grace in its various forms.
1 Peter 4:10

AUTHOR'S REFLECTIONS

Warriors don't worry. They don't go through life fretting about tomorrow. This is especially true — or should be true — of God's warriors. We can be assured of tomorrow and free from the fear of death or famine or sickness, because we know how powerful the God of the Angel-Armies is. The Captain of the Hosts is on our side and with Him on our side, even death cannot be victorious against us.

If we ask for it, we receive the faith to face tomorrow with boldness, strength, and courage. We can serve others and pour out the gifts we have received from Him with abandon, because we are confident He will not allow us to ever be lacking in what we need. We can be brave because we can go into battle against the enemy of our soul, trusting that no weapon forged against us will prosper, and in our obedience and sacrifice, there is a reward waiting for us.

Our God is a Rewarder. We may not grab hold of it in this life, but we will surely discover it in the laden treasures we have stored up in the heavens.

day 33

An Unlikely Home

The warrior bride had never imagined herself living in a lavish palace, with her every need met, nothing lacking, nothing missing. Something about the extravagance surrounding her unsettled her. Somehow, it reminded her of the King's humble beginnings, of mangers, and inns with no room for travelers. For some reason, the warrior bride yearned for the home and hearth of Lady Wisdom, for the Academy of Light, for places that felt closer to home than this palace. Why did she feel this way? Shouldn't she be comfortable in the palace of the King? Where was the King, anyway? When could she see Him?

The scarlet woman had provided her with very little information and had deflected whenever the warrior bride pried her for answers. Left alone to wait for the company of Faith and the iron maiden, the warrior bride desired the presence of the Lover of souls. She could still sense His heartbeat against her chest — how much He loved the kingdom's citizens — the same love He had allowed her to experience for her people.

A deep loneliness filled her, so when someone knocked on her door, she was more than ready to welcome the company of her friends.

"Isn't it lovely?!" Faith exclaimed as she flitted around the vast room. "This room alone is bigger than the entire inn at the city of darkness!"

The warrior bride bristled at the mention of the city where she had died, but she hadn't died, had she? Shouldn't she be more jubilant?

The iron maiden gave her a tight hug. "We thought we had lost you. The sacrifice you have given for the kingdom will not be forgotten. You certainly deserve all the rewards, acclaim, and glory coming to you."

It was the last statement from the iron maiden that tuned in the warrior bride on something amiss. This didn't seem like something her fellow leader would say. After all, it wasn't glory, acclaim, or reward they were after. It had always been their heart to bring glory and pleasure to the King, and His presence felt sorely absent here.

"What happened?" the warrior bride asked.

"The short of it is that you died and awakened to your just reward," Faith said. "Now, in the absence of the King, while we await His return, you are to rule His kingdom."

This unsettled the warrior bride even more, though a prideful part of her desired all of this to be true. It appealed to her vanity; however, the warrior bride backed away from her friends and narrowed her eyes at them. "Where are we really?"

Wherever they were, it couldn't possibly be her King's home, because it certainly didn't feel like hers.

Manna

VERSES FOR MEDITATION

MARY — RISKED: *and she gave birth to her firstborn, a son. She wrapped him in cloths and placed him in a manger, because there was no guest room available for them.*
Luke 2:7

How can you believe since you accept glory from one another but do not seek the glory that comes from the only God?
John 5:44

Not to us, LORD, not to us but to your name be the glory, because of your love and faithfulness.
Psalm 115:1

Whoever speaks, as one who speaks oracles of God; whoever serves, as one who serves by the strength that God supplies—in order that in everything God may be glorified through Jesus Christ. To him belong glory and dominion forever and ever. Amen.
1 Peter 4:11

AUTHOR'S REFLECTIONS

It is both astounding and breathtaking to remember how humble a life Jesus lived here on earth. One would think the God of the universe would introduce His Son to the world with more glory and extravagance than a full inn and a manger. From the beginning of his life, it seemed the world could not make room for him. Yet, He came in all humility, the King of Kings.

In this life, one of the greatest battles we must find ourselves victorious over is the subtle lure of comfort and complacency. This is a trap many Christians — especially those in Christian countries — can fall into. The prosperity gospel is rampant, and we have leaders in the faith living extravagant lives while failing to store for themselves treasures in heaven, which is of far greater worth than any treasure we build up here on earth.

God surely wants to bless His children, and He has promised us blessed lives in His Word, but when this becomes the aim rather than a means for us to further align ourselves with His purposes and further His kingdom, we may be in danger of straying from the heart of Christianity: in Him, with Him, to Him is where we belong. Jesus is our home.

day 34

TREASURES OF THE HEART

The mirage flickered, faltered, and faded away. In its place was a bright light, blinding the warrior bride's eyes. She was no longer in some extravagant palace but in the open air, above ground, taking flight.

She blinked her eyes to get a better look at her surroundings. A strength she was familiar with was supporting her. As her vision readjusted, the face of an ally became clear. The red-winged warrior was carrying her in the air. She smiled at him.

"You're awake." The relief in his voice was unmistakable.

"What happened?"

"They put the sword through you, and you fell to the ground. With your last breath, the prince of darkness declared victory."

The memory of the sword going through her brought a sharp pain in her gut. She groaned. She touched her stomach and found a moist spot where the sword had gone through. Blood.

"They were about to drag you out of the platform, but the moment they tried to, a great light burst out of you. It was blinding." His face was as a flint as he glided through the air, carrying her in his arms. "More than that, it pierced the darkness. It was unlike anything any of us have ever experienced before. The light revealed the darkness in all of us."

The warrior bride hung on his every word. What had the King done through her death?

"The prince was furious, but it was chaos after. There wasn't much he could do, especially when the light caused the scales from the eyes and ears of those present to fall. The blind can see. The deaf can hear. It was stunning. You truly are a daughter of light."

A surge of gratefulness swelled in her heart. "The light wasn't mine at all, but the King's. You believe me, don't you?"

"After what I've seen, how can I not believe? I envy those who believed even when they haven't yet seen. Like my brother."

"Where is your brother?"

"He is accompanying the sentinel and the iron maiden as they take everyone who wishes to leave the city of darkness to the kingdom of light. There are many who have chosen to become sojourners, citizens of light instead of darkness."

The news delighted the warrior bride's heart, but why then weren't they in the company of those whom the King had entrusted under her care?

"Why are we apart from them? Where are we going?" she asked.

"The sentinel and iron maiden decided it would be best for me to take you to the kingdom of light ahead of everyone else, so you can receive proper treatment."

"No." The warrior bride shook her head. "Take me back."

"You are weak and wounded. You need a physician."

"Take me back to them. The adversary has tried to keep me distracted with mirages and delusions, but the mission is not yet complete. The people are still in darkness. I cannot rest until I have seen them brought into light."

Understanding flickered in the sharp gaze of the winged one, whom she was certain had now become a solid ally she could rely on. Without another word of objection, he shifted direction and turned back to restore the shepherd to her sheep.

Manna

VERSES FOR MEDITATION

MARY — RISKED: *But Mary treasured up all these things and pondered them in her heart.*
Luke 2:19

*The people walking in darkness
have seen a great light;
on those living in the land of deep darkness
a light has dawned.*
Isaiah 9:2

For God, who said, "Let light shine out of darkness," made his light shine in our hearts to give us the light of the knowledge of God's glory displayed in the face of Christ.
2 Corinthians 4:6

Therefore let us move beyond the elementary teachings about Christ and be taken forward to maturity, not laying again the foundation of repentance from acts that lead to death, and of faith in God
Hebrews 6:1

AUTHOR'S REFLECTIONS

Take note of those who are in service to the King — the ones who are on fire, passionate, and focused on the calling and purpose God has placed upon their lives. They are tenacious and relentless.

They know they live for a higher purpose and calling. Their walk with God is not limited to their own needs and concerns being met.

Their prayers no longer go inward, but outward. They are fighting for their families, their cities, their nations, the world.

They are assured of their salvation and walk blamelessly before the Lord, not because of their own efforts against sin, but because they are constantly in pursuit of God.

The Apostle Paul encourages us to move beyond the elementary teachings of Christ and "be taken forward" to maturity. How are we cooperating with the Holy Spirit and applying the Word so we can progress into maturity in Christ?

DARING ESCAPES

They reached their friends right before the much larger company of people was about to approach the walls of the city. The mere sight of them brought a smile to the warrior bride's face. Her heart ached for each of those present — even the ones she hadn't even met yet. A mixture of surprise and delight crossed the faces of her fellow kingdom sojourners, the sentinel and the iron maiden.

"Why did you bring her back?" the sentinel asked the winged warrior. "She is yet unwell and needs looking after."

"I insisted," the warrior bride said. "I need to see our mission through. To finish what we began together."

"You have done more than enough for this mission," the iron maiden said. "Surely, the King can acknowledge that and reward you for what you've already done."

"That may be so—" the warrior bride smiled as she tried to steady herself on the ground, her knees still wobbly from flight "—but I want to stay the course and finish. Besides, we are close to the end, and the prince of darkness will have no choice but to honor the deal he made with me. He must give us safe passage past the city gates and back to kingdom territory."

The sentinel and the iron maiden exchanged glances and smiled upon realizing there was no way for them to dissuade the warrior bride from the course of action she had chosen. After being welcomed by the rest of their group — sharing a hug with the scarlet woman who profusely thanked her once again — the warrior bride and her people proceeded past the gates of the city of darkness without further resistance.

It had been about half a day's walk past the city gates when the kingdom capital appeared on the horizon. They were close! Rejoicing filled their company as they all accelerated their pace forward.

Whatever joy the warrior bride felt was disrupted when a familiar hiss rang in her ear. She gritted her teeth, though at this point, the voice of her adversary was more an annoyance than an actual threat.

<u>You have taken what's mine. These wrongdoers and transgressors have no place in a kingdom so full of pride over their own righteousness. They will come right back to the darkness, because stains have no business being around purity. You are imperfect yourself. What makes you think you can be a worthy match to the King? You think you've thwarted the delusions of your mind? No! You are still deluded. You—</u>

The scarlet woman — once a daughter of enmity; now, a daughter of blessing — rushed beside the warrior bride and stomped her foot on the ground, immediately silencing the slithering voice.

The warrior bride looked down and saw a snake's head crushed beneath her feet.

She smiled. "That's enough of that, right? We already escaped sin and death. We can escape the lies the darkness sends, as well."

The warrior bride returned the daughter of blessing's smile. They held hands, and alongside them, everyone else clasped their hands with one another's. Together, they all marched forward and entered the kingdom of light, united as one.

Mission accomplished.

Manna

VERSES FOR MEDITATION

MARY — RISKED: *When they had gone, an angel of the Lord appeared to Joseph in a dream. "Get up," he said, "take the child and his mother and escape to Egypt. Stay there until I tell you, for Herod is going to search for the child to kill him."*
Matthew 2:13

He has saved us and called us to a holy life—not because of anything we have done but because of his own purpose and grace. This grace was given us in Christ Jesus before the beginning of time, but it has now been revealed through the appearing of our Savior, Christ Jesus, who has destroyed death and has brought life and immortality to light through the gospel.
2 Timothy 1:9-10

But he who endures to the end shall be saved. And this gospel of the kingdom will be preached in all the world as a witness to all the nations, and then the end will come.
Matthew 24:13-14 (NKJV)

But I do not account my life of any value nor as precious to myself, if only I may finish my course and the ministry that I received from the Lord Jesus, to testify to the gospel of the grace of God.
Acts 20:24 (ESV)

AUTHOR'S REFLECTIONS

"It is finished."

This is what Jesus uttered on the cross before He took his last breath. He accomplished what He had come to earth to accomplish, and what a great and complete work it was! In doing so, He redeemed us from the consequences of the choice made by the woman who first sinned and crushed the enemy with His heel.

Just as He accomplished His work, we too have our own purpose to fulfill, our own work to accomplish here on earth while we still have breath in us. There is yet the Great Commission. Many yet need to hear the Gospel.

According to the *Joshua Project*, over three billion people, 41.8% of the world's population — over *a third of us* — are still unreached. This means they haven't yet heard the Gospel. This is a staggering number, and it is a picture of how much work we still have ahead of us.

What is your role in fulfilling the Great Commission and reaching the unreached? How are you taking part in the great work Jesus left all Christians to accomplish?

day 36

A Fragrant Bride

The moment they entered the kingdom capital, its citizens welcomed their arrival with great joy and celebration. A parade had been prepared for them, as the warrior bride was to be brought into the palace of the King to be made ready to present herself to Him at His throne room.

Many familiar faces were part of the entourage tasked with bringing the warrior bride to the palace. Faith was delighted upon getting reunited with her friends from the wilderness — the gossamer prince and princess and the troubadour among them. Lady Wisdom was there too and was the first to approach the warrior bride.

"You have arrived victorious." Delight flickered in her eyes as she brushed a finger against the hair of the warrior bride. "You have come so far! There's much to celebrate before you start your preparations."

"Preparations?"

"You will need to be ready before you can meet with the King. For now, there is a great feast awaiting you and your friends. I'm sure you are hungry and tired after the harrowing journey." Lady Wisdom frowned at the bandages around the warrior bride's waist. "We will see to that as well. Right now, the citizens of the Great King's city welcomes you!"

The days that followed were one of joyous reunions and jubilant feasting. The warrior bride's wards — the scarlet woman and the winged brothers included — had taken on their childlike forms and entered the Academy of Light, under the wing of Lady Wisdom herself. The sentinel and the iron maiden accompanied the warrior bride in the palace as her friends and advisers, each of them having given their own positions in the King's court. Faith chose to stay behind as well and not return to the wilderness with their winged friends.

The period of peace that came was a welcome reprieve from the battles of the wilderness, the training of the academy, and the manipulations of the city of darkness. The peace, however, was momentary, for there was still a great work to be done, and the warrior bride's preparations for meeting with the King were about to commence.

On the first day of her year of preparation, the warrior bride didn't know what to expect, but she had determined early on to surrender herself to the process. She was about to completely shed away who she once was and embrace who she had to be to rule and reign with the King.

And so, it began — the anointing of myrrh and perfumes, as well as everything necessary for a beautiful bride to emerge — one whose very presence would provide a pleasing fragrance before the King.

Manna

VERSES FOR MEDITATION

BRIDE — BETROTHED: *Each young woman's turn came to go in to King Ahasuerus after she had completed twelve months' preparation, according to the regulations for the women, for thus were the days of their preparation apportioned: six months with oil of myrrh, and six months with perfumes and preparations for beautifying women.*
Esther 2:12 (NKJV)

"Or suppose a woman has ten silver coins and loses one. Doesn't she light a lamp, sweep the house and search carefully until she finds it? And when she finds it, she calls her friends and neighbors together and says, 'Rejoice with me; I have found my lost coin.' In the same way, I tell you, there is rejoicing in the presence of the angels of God over one sinner who repents."
Luke 15:8-10

Our lives are a Christ-like fragrance rising up to God. But this fragrance is perceived differently by those who are being saved and by those who are perishing.
2 Corinthians 2:15

AUTHOR'S REFLECTIONS

Our time as part of God's kingdom isn't all battles and challenges, trials and sacrifices. The God of the Sabbath surely is one Who knows how to give His children rest. He is a God Who delights in laughing with us, feasting with us, being at rest with us.

As we go through our Christian walk, we learn to recognize and discern moments of feasting and moments of fasting, seasons of warring and seasons of peace. We learn when to fight and when to retreat, when to play and when to work.

Everything in its perfect time — in His time.

Is there anything in your life right now you feel is worth celebrating and thanking God for? What can you do to glorify God and cultivate awareness of His presence in your seasons of satisfaction and rejoicing?

day 37

A Ready Bride

Day in and day out, the life of the warrior bride fell into a routine, a schedule, a timeline. With each day passing, her yearning for the King grew, even if she had made a practice out of cultivating an awareness of His presence with her at all times.

One such morning, as she immersed herself in the regimen of beautification assigned to her at the palace, the yearning in her heart for her Beloved had become almost unbearable. She knew the time was drawing nigh, and she longed for that day, but no one knew the exact day and hour.

The process had been painful at times, as it meant scrubbing away — sometimes burning away — remnants of her old self. The wilderness and all her kingdom exploits had molded the warrior bride for this season of pruning, however. She was ready to be made ready.

Months flew by and despite her routine, she made an effort to keep alert and stay awake for the day of His arrival. Every morning, she would step out into the terraces of the palace to watch for her King's return. Every evening, before she lay her head to sleep, she would do the same thing.

Her friends kept her company and updated her on everything happening in the kingdom. Many ministered to her whenever she felt faint or in need of encouragement.

Finally, the day came.

She had just gone through her daily purification process when the iron maiden and the sentinel approached her with faces full of glee.

"He is coming!" the iron maiden exclaimed. "He is on His way to the palace! It is time!"

The sentinel spoke in a much calmer and more level tone, but the anticipation in his expressions was unmistakable. "You will be presented before Him at His throne room the moment He summons you."

The warrior bride's heart skipped a beat. This was the moment she had been preparing for. Her smile grew wide even as she realized she was ready for this. Her anticipation grew and her soul rested in the knowledge that she was His, and His desire was for her. After all, hadn't He taken her through the wilderness into His kingdom? Hadn't He rescued her from sure death in the city of darkness?

Yes, she embraced who she was. She was His beloved. She had nothing to fear.

Manna

VERSES FOR MEDITATION

BRIDE — BETROTHED: *Thus prepared, each young woman went to the king, and she was given whatever she desired to take with her from the women's quarters to the king's palace.*
Esther 2:13 (NKJV)

I belong to my beloved, and his desire is for me.
Song of Solomon 7:10

*Let us rejoice and be glad
and give him glory!
For the wedding of the Lamb has come,
and his bride has made herself ready.
Fine linen, bright and clean,
was given her to wear."
(Fine linen stands for the righteous acts of God's holy people.)*
Revelation 19:7-8

Therefore keep watch, because you do not know the day or the hour.
Matthew 20:13

AUTHOR'S REFLECTIONS

We can sometimes get lost in the routine and the mundane rigmarole of Christian living, thinking our faithfulness and obedience through every day of our lives are overlooked or unseen. Worst of all, we may think it doesn't matter or has no impact.

Let's not forget there is beauty in submitting ourselves to the daily disciplines of a faithful Christian walk, whether we see the fruit in it or not. We keep going; we persevere; we stay faithful. This is what we are called to do, and we pour our time and our lives into it, but this doesn't mean we don't stay alert.

We must be as the five wise virgins who kept their lamps ready with the oil of the Holy Spirit, alert and watchful, knowing the signs and the times, so when the King returns, we are not caught by surprise.

We have remained ablaze for our First Love — neither cold nor lukewarm, but on fire — anticipating being in the presence of our Beloved, crying out, Maranatha! Lord, come!

What are you doing to make yourself ready — pure and holy — for the return of Jesus Christ?

day 38

A Humble Bride

Faith and the iron maiden were beside themselves with excitement as they rushed inside the warrior bride's bedroom. She chuckled as she exchanged looks with the sentinel, whose affection and admiration for her was unmistakable.

"We've come a long way from when we were first kingdom children on a mission," he said.

"We have." The warrior bride nodded. "There'll be more missions to look forward to. There is much yet that needs to be done."

"We await how the King will direct you and us, but for now, we get to enjoy His company and take part in His fellowship." His eyes sparkled with a burning love for the King and the kingdom even as he lifted his chin up with pride that he belonged to this kingdom. "It has been an honor serving the King with you, princess."

"An honor and a pleasure for me, as well," the warrior bride said.

"Come now!" Faith called out to her. "There's much that needs to be done! Your handmaidens are on their way. We must clothe you with splendor. You will look glorious once you are presented before the King."

"I need not present myself with extravagance." The warrior bride waved the sentinel goodbye and entered her bedroom to join her sisters. "The King owns everything, and I can offer Him nothing other than myself. Fine linen, clean and bright, will do. He will welcome me as I am, and I will leave His presence as He wants me to be."

The iron maiden's eyes moistened. "You are at the palace for such a time as this, I am sure of it. You are right. We must collect ourselves and figure out what is pleasing to the King and not rely on our own thinking of how things should be."

The hours flew by, and they spent it washing the warrior bride with water, putting ointments on her, and dressing her in embroidery, fine linen, and silk. They adorned her with jewelry and placed sandals of fine leather on her feet.

When time came to present her before the King, she was radiant in her beauty, but there was yet one thing missing — something to offer the King.

It was the iron maiden's idea, for it had been her who had kept the weapon from the city of darkness. She handed the sharp sword to the warrior bride, who gasped at the sight of it. "Is this—"

"Yes." The iron maiden nodded. "The very same one that took your life from you, only for His light to shine on you and bring you back to life anew. I'm sure the King will know what it signifies."

The warrior bride clutched the hilt of the sword in her hand as she perused herself in the mirror and barely recognized her reflection compared to the woman who had taken her first steps through the wilderness. At her radiance, not a hint of pride could be found within her — only gratefulness, because it was Him. She was her Beloved's handiwork. All she had done was get out of the way and allow Him to mold her as He pleased.

Manna

VERSES FOR MEDITATION

BRIDE — BETROTHED: *Now when the turn came for Esther the daughter of Abihail the uncle of Mordecai, who had taken her as his daughter, to go in to the king, she requested nothing but what Hegai the king's eunuch, the custodian of the women, advised. And Esther obtained favor in the sight of all who saw her.*
Esther 2:15

*Wealth and honor come from you;
you are the ruler of all things.
In your hands are strength and power
to exalt and give strength to all...
But who am I, and who are my people, that we should
be able to give as generously as this? Everything comes
from you, and we have given you only what comes from
your hand.*
1 Chronicles 29:12,14

*Husbands, love your wives, just as Christ loved the
church and gave himself up for her to make her holy,
cleansing her by the washing with water through the
word, and to present her to himself as a radiant church,
without stain or wrinkle or any other blemish, but holy
and blameless.*
Ephesians 5:25-27

AUTHOR'S REFLECTIONS

In *Mere Christianity*, C. S. Lewis said, "Humility is not thinking less of yourself, it's thinking of yourself less." This selflessness and willingness to give ourselves away for the sake of His kingdom and His glory marks the kind of Bride our Savior is coming back for.

The world is increasingly becoming selfish. It's all about us, all about being the best, the most beautiful, the most desirable, but Scripture tells us to be set apart, to be the ones who would turn the other cheek, who would be gentle when others are abrasive, kind when others are forceful.

If we are to present ourselves before Christ as holy, blameless, and without blemish, we need to learn to be humble, to acknowledge that everything we have is not from us and not for us. God has given us all we have, so we may offer it back to Him by using what He has given for the good of His kingdom and His people.

Let's take time today to focus on Him and seek His heart and mind. Only by setting our eyes on Him and allowing Him to be Lord over our lives can we renew our mind to think more about God, His kingdom, and His glory rather than just our own wants, needs, and desires.

day 39

A Confident Bride

The warrior bride walked past the halls and gardens of the palace, an entourage behind her, supporting her, cheering her on. Her heartbeat sped up in anticipation as she made her way past the outer and inner courts. Everyone else stayed behind when they reached the torn veil. She was to meet with him alone.

As she awaited His summons, she took a deep breath. Her smile grew at the notion of the King calling for her, choosing her. She could respond with nothing but delight even as images of the sweet encounters she had with Him flashed through her mind.

The seconds ticked by and the last thing she would have expected to hear at the courts of the King was the familiar slither of her adversary lingering in her mind.

"The light of His glory will kill you. What makes you think you are prepared enough for such an encounter? Your radiance pales compared to His."

Right as the unwanted voice of accusation flitted through her head, the recollection of the daughter of blessing crushing a snake's head with her heel revisited the warrior bride's thoughts. She laughed. She had faced death once already and had been transformed into a new creation. There was nothing to worry about, nothing to fear. She was exactly where she needed to be, where she belonged.

The doors to the throne room swung open, and she entered, unflinching. Her face radiant, her gaze focused on none but the King, she strode in with full confidence in His ability to make her worthy of this encounter. Upon reaching the foot of His throne, she bowed before Him, and He extended His scepter of strength to her — a sign of His approval. She laid down her sword at His feet.

"ARISE, WARRIOR BRIDE," the King said. "LIFT UP YOUR FACE."

She did as she was told. Though she still could not see His face behind the radiance streaming from the throne down to her, she sensed His pleasure and His smile.

"YOU ARE ALTOGETHER BEAUTIFUL, MY DARLING."

Her eyes moistened at His words even as she trembled at the glory of His presence. A deep reverence took over her, once faced with His majesty.

"COME," He said. "THE TIME OF JUDGMENT AND SORTING OUT HASN'T YET ARRIVED. WE ARE STILL IN A TIME OF MERCY AND GRACE, AND THE WORLD BEYOND MY KINGDOM IS IN GREAT NEED OF A SAVIOR. LINGER HERE WITH ME. LET US DISCUSS WHAT LIES AHEAD."

Thus, in the presence of the King, she lingered and listened. They discussed and reasoned together, and it delighted her heart that He would trust her with His kingdom strategies, as He would trust a friend.

She could have stayed there with Him for eternity, but for now, all she could do was linger for as long as He would permit before sending her out again to bring His presence for the world beyond to experience His glory shining through her.

Manna

VERSES FOR MEDITATION

BRIDE — BETROTHED: *And Mordecai told them to answer Esther: "Do not think in your heart that you will escape in the king's palace any more than all the other Jews. For if you remain completely silent at this time, relief and deliverance will arise for the Jews from another place, but you and your father's house will perish. Yet who knows whether you have come to the kingdom for such a time as this?"*

Then Esther told them to reply to Mordecai: ...if I perish, I perish!"
Esther 4:13–16c

When the Son of Man comes in his glory, and all the angels with him, he will sit on his glorious throne. All the nations will be gathered before him, and he will separate the people one from another as a shepherd separates the sheep from the goats.
Matthew 20:31-32

She is clothed with strength and dignity, and she laughs without fear of the future.
Proverbs 31:25 (NLT)

Let us then approach God's throne of grace with confidence, so that we may receive mercy and find grace to help us in our time of need.
Hebrews 4:16

AUTHOR'S REFLECTIONS

As we mature in Him, we get to a point when He begins to entrust us with His plans and strategies.

We are no longer foot soldiers, but partakers in legislating and executing His rule and authority in the places He has entrusted to us.

Few of us reach the point Abraham reached where he was referred to as the friend of God, able to negotiate with God over the fate of cities (i.e. Sodom and Gomorrah). Let us, however, desire to reach that point of maturity in our walk with God, because though we still live in a time of mercy and grace — not judgment — the time is short. It will benefit the church to be aware of God's mind, God's plans and strategies in this day and age.

The Bride of Christ will one day rule and reign with Him, and she cannot be called ready if she yet cannot be trusted by Him.

Can God entrust you with His secrets? Are you a friend of God? This selflessness and willingness to give ourselves away for the sake of His kingdom and His glory marks the kind of Bride our Savior is coming back for.

The Kingdom Call

Whether it took hours or days, it didn't matter. The warrior bride wasn't about to leave His presence without receiving everything she could from Him. In the light of His presence, she could sense it, how hearing about His plans and getting glimpses of His heart and mind was transforming her. She relished every moment spent with Him, and the time for her to be sent out yet again had come too soon, but it was inevitable, because there was much yet to be done, more territories where His glorious kingdom yet required advancing.

"TAKE UP YOUR SWORD, WARRIOR BRIDE," the King instructed. "YOUR ADVERSARY MEANT IT FOR YOUR HARM, BUT IT HAS INSTEAD GIVEN YOU A BRAND NEW LIFE. CLOTHE YOURSELF IN FULL ARMOR. DO NOT FORGET ALL YOU HAVE LEARNED AND PREPARE AS MANY AS YOU CAN FOR MY RETURN. GO TO THE ENDS OF THE EARTH, AND THEN COME BACK TO ME. NO MATTER WHERE YOU ARE, YOU CAN ALWAYS COME HOME TO ME. MAKE SURE EVERYONE HEARS ABOUT IT. I AM COMING BACK, AND ONCE I DO, WE SHALL RULE AND REIGN TOGETHER."

His instructions still lingered in her mind as the warrior bride walked out of His throne room with a brand new sense of purpose and a determination to fulfill His

Great Commission. The gathering of the children of light had to continue before darkness could take over.

She stepped out into the terraces and drank in the view of the kingdom before her. It was shining with His brilliant glory, but beyond the light, there yet was a world cloaked in darkness. This time, she wasn't about to go out into the world on her own, but with an army like her — one in heart and in mind — ready and willing to surrender their lives even unto death if it meant more would hear and see of the return of the King of Glory.

Someday, His government would be established in the kingdom and beyond. Until then, the warrior bride continued to contend.

Manna

VERSES FOR MEDITATION

BRIDE — BETROTHED: *The Spirit and the bride say, "Come!" And let the one who hears say, "Come!" Let the one who is thirsty come; and let the one who wishes take the free gift of the water of life.*
Revelation 22:17

But as for you, you meant evil against me; but God meant it for good, in order to bring it about as it is this day, to save many people alive.
Genesis 50:20 (NKJV)

*Of the greatness of his government and peace there will be no end.
He will reign on David's throne and over his kingdom,
establishing and upholding it with justice and righteousness from that time on and forever.
The zeal of the Lord Almighty will accomplish this.*
Isaiah 9:7

AUTHOR'S REFLECTIONS

This is the last entry, the last day of this series of devotionals. As much as I would want it to, this devotional cannot end with a wedding feast, because the story of the Bride and the Lamb is yet unfolding. We are part of this story, and we have a role to play in all of it. I hope this devotional has been another reminder of the need for us to be prepared as we await the King's return.

I pray that, at the very least, it will awaken in you a desire to know more about what it means to be a part of the Bride of Christ. May it enrich your understanding of the church's role in these last days. May it kindle a flame with you to help fulfill the Great Commission. Finally, may it be a reminder that we must prepare ourselves — without blemish — so we can be found holy and acceptable unto God when Christ returns.

God bless you on your journey! May you stay ablaze with love for God, the Church, and the lost until He returns. Until then, keep contending! Maranatha!

the author

BELOVED

Joanna Alonzo is an author of Christian fiction novels with grit, grace, and wonder. She has a Bachelor's Degree in Information Technology from St. Louis University, but her creative leanings drew her away from software development to a career in faith and uncertainty. Her homebase is La Trinidad Valley in the Philippines, but she wanders around too much to have a permanent residence. She is a fascinated apprentice to the Greatest Storyteller of all and loves to highlight His supernatural grace in her stories. She loves having coffee chats with people, but isn't a fan of them hugging her too much. Find out more about her and her work at WWW.JOANNATHEPARADOX.COM.

joannatheparadox

HINENI PUBLISHING

Hineni (יננה) is a Hebrew word that means "Here am I" or "Here I am". It's how Abraham, Moses, Samuel, and Isaiah responded to the voice of the Lord when He called on them. It denotes not a presentation of ourselves as ready and totally available.

Hineni Publishing is a Philippine-based Christian company established in 2020. The heart and vision of Hineni Publishing is to produce books and literature written by "a ready scribe" seeking to please the King as in Psalm 45:1 - "My heart overflows with a pleasing theme; I address my verses to the king; my tongue is like the pen of a ready scribe." (ESV)

www.ingramcontent.com/pod-product-compliance
Lightning Source LLC
Chambersburg PA
CBHW051438130726
47987CB00005B/2104